PRA
HEARTIFI

"In *Heartificial Empathy,* Minter Dial masterfully makes the case for why empathy is not only teachable but a requirement for success in business and in life. By dissecting the elements of empathy, Dial has created the recipe book of how to embed and increase empathy in yourself, your organization, and in our machines."

– **Charlene Li**, best-selling author and founder of Altimeter, a Prophet company

"Minter Dial is onto something. Everyone talks about the need for empathy in business and society, but no one describes what that would look like. Dial takes a great first stab at envisioning a future in which deliberate empathy drives both business success and greater societal cohesion. A must-read for forward-thinking leaders everywhere."

– **Marty Neumeier**, author of *Metaskills* and *The Brand Gap*

"Empathy will be the key competitive advantage of the twenty-first century. Dial captures the fullest essence of that one special quality that makes us truly human. Dial skillfully illustrates how we can industrialise meaningful solutions for human happiness."

– **Nell Watson**, Artificial Intelligence & Robotics faculty, Singularity University, cofounder of EthicsNet

"The most engaging storytellers are systematically loaded with empathy. They not only relate on a personal level, but they vicariously experience the feelings of their audience to achieve a deeper connection. In *Heartificial Empathy*, Minter Dial has crafted a rich study of the importance of empathy for business, centered around personal experience, technology, and the coming age of spiritual machines. A must-read for business leaders and those in charge of AI initiatives."

– **Jason Miller**, Brand Marketing Lead, EMEA – Microsoft Advertising / Bing

"In a tech-driven society, empathy is an increasingly rare and valuable skill. Minter Dial's new book is a thought-provoking exploration of the role of empathy in the modern workplace, and how to nurture and sustain it."

– **Dorie Clark**, author of *Entrepreneurial You* and *Stand Out*

"In a world where emerging technologies, such as artificial intelligence, will play an ever more pervasive role in our lives, Minter Dial makes an urgent and compelling case for the need for that most human of traits – empathy – to be prioritised.

This will not simply be a nice-to-have for businesses, but will be an essential ingredient in how they responsibly engage with the communities they serve in the future."

– **Rob McCargow**, director of Artificial Intelligence, PwC United Kingdom

"In *Heartificial Empathy*, Minter Dial probes some interesting questions: Can we develop empathy – in people, leaders, organizations, and (interestingly) machines? The truth is that it's not only possible . . . it's essential."

– **Ann Handley**, *Wall Street Journal* best-selling author and chief content officer, MarketingProfs

"Finally, Minter Dial brings all the facets and research of empathy into modern context. This read is an enthralling and sweeping journey along the trajectory of empathy for leadership, society and the sciences. The ultimate vision is one where we are catapulted into the future to 'artificial empathy,' where artificial intelligence can be an unexpectedly noble and pragmatic way to feed our human souls."

– **Marie R. Miyashiro**, author, *The Empathy Factor*

"In this thought-provoking book, Minter will help you to navigate your way through the hype surrounding AI, while driving you with the inevitable conclusion that the best combination is (and always will be) a good human *and* a machine."

– **Jeremy Waite**, chief strategy officer, IBM Watson customer engagement

"Up until now, we've seen technologists focus on the raw mechanics of what artificial intelligence can do. But what if we applied that computing expertise to the most powerful lever of customer loyalty and long-term profitability? Putting more empathy into our teams, tools, and processes can only result in vastly better experiences."

– **Scott Monty**, principal & founder, Scott Monty Strategies

"In his spellbinding new book, Minter Dial shares a treasure trove of ideas and academic insights that explain empathy and its impact on people and businesses. He explores machine-based empathy. How might that work? Could ethical frameworks be hardcoded into transactional, digital systems? What are the challenges, the opportunities and the limitations? This beautifully crafted work will open your mind to possibilities. You will learn about the future and the world that awaits. Armed with this knowledge, you stand a much better chance of shaping it to your advantage."

– **Rod Banner**, entrepreneur, investor and passionate instigator of JoyTech.org

"A must-read for business and technical folks alike."

– **Phil Harvey**, coauthor of *Data: A Guide to Humans*

Heartificial **Empathy**

OTHER BOOKS BY MINTER DIAL

Futureproof: How to Get Your Business Ready for the Next Disruption, cowritten with Caleb Storkey (Pearson Financial Times Press, 2017)

- Winner of Business Book Award 2018, category: Embracing Change.
- Available as e-book (Kindle) and paperback.
- Find out more at www.futureproof.ly.

The Last Ring Home: A POW's Lasting Legacy of Courage, Love and Honor in World War II (Myndset Press, 2016)

- Winner of Book Excellence Award 2018, category: Biography.
- Available as audiobook (Audible), e-book (Kindle) and hardcover.
- Find out more at www.thelastringhome.com.

Heartificial **Empathy**

Putting Heart into Business and Artificial Intelligence

An in-depth look at empathy:
how it is created; why and how
to increase empathy in people,
organisations and machines;
and the flaws to be avoided

Minter Dial

With Illustrations by Joel Anderson Waithe

Dear Ed,
With heartfelt thanks
and continued enthusiasm
for Empathy Week!
Hugs, Minter Dial
15/4/2020

To report errors or request permissions,
contact publisher@digitalproof.co.

Publisher: DigitalProof Press
Cover design and design production: Minter Dial
Illustrations: Joel Anderson Waithe
ISBN 978-1916480902
www.minterdial.com

Figure 1 – Mr. E's superpower: putting heart into everything

Illustration by Joel Anderson Waithe

CONTENTS

FIGURES

PREFACE

Can Machines Help Us Become Better Humans?

Do you think you'll ever fall in love with a machine?

Do you think you'll ever feel close to one?

Do you think machines will ever display believable feelings?

There was a time when I didn't believe so, either. Things have changed, and I have evidence.

These questions bring up important opportunities and threats for business and for society at large. As fast as the pace of change has been, it's only going to get faster. Despite its breakneck speed – if we want our businesses to survive and thrive – we *have* to learn to keep up with it. And the critical value and skill that will help us do that is empathy. Astute business leaders will start to look for alternative methods to build their empathic muscles. Artificial Intelligence (AI) will necessarily be part of that equation as we learn to bake in artificial empathy. I pray that, when and as we get there, it will be genuine and heartfelt – call it *heartificial* – empathy.

The world seems to be in a spiral of never-ending crises. Will we, as enlightened human beings, be able to resolve the division, hostility and incivility that plague us, or will the animal in us win out? Or will the machine ultimately prevail? The world is undergoing seismic change, and we need to adapt or suffer the consequences. Our brains, business models and societal norms all need to be rewired and rethought. Our society needs a major empathy upgrade. Are we equipped for the new challenges? Each generation of human beings always feels they are special and distinct: "*This* time it's different." But surely there *are* some major differences in the revolution currently underway. If there's any reassurance, it's that human beings have great skills of adaptation. We've gone through massive change before.

The sixth-century BC Greek philosopher Heraclitus asserted that "change is the only constant." Even the divisive political climate in the US we're seeing today was felt in the past with a similar vehemence. At least my great-grandfather, US senator from South Carolina Nathaniel Barksdale Dial, said as much in a speech he delivered on the Senate floor in 1924:

> I'm thoroughly disgusted by the way the government in Washington "works." There is almost

> total partisanship, both on the right and the left . . . neither side talks to the other, and . . . the divide just seems to be getting worse. . . . Self-interest comes before the national interest. By self-interest I don't just mean the interest a representative may or may not have for his constituents, I also mean the desire to hang onto his job and all of its salary and benefits. I find the whole thing pretty pathetic.[1]

The more things change, the more things stay the same. The eternal optimist in me would like to believe we can and should hope for better. The pragmatic realist in me, however, warns that it won't happen through wishful thinking. We must act. And if we don't strive for enlightenment and progress, we may end up with a more dour version of ourselves, played out through robots that are superior to us. Each of us has a role to play as we experience and "enjoy" this fascinating period of change. As Caleb Storkey and I wrote about in chapter two of *Futureproof*, I need to emphasise the importance of self-responsibility. I'm adamant that we must own the solution and be sufficiently self-aware to recognise our role in the problem.[2]

Gregg Hurwitz, the *New York Times* best-selling author and self-assessed classical liberal, said in a podcast with the conservative Dr. Jordan Peterson that we should seek to create an environment where "people can be free to make choices and perform at a level that they want to build their whole future."[3] There is, in his statement, the premise for a new social "operating system." So-called liberals and conservatives have complementary skills that need one another. While conservatives could develop more empathy, the challenge for liberals, given their predisposition to "higher" empathy, is to stay humble. It behoves both sides to learn to reach out to the other.

Few industries and sectors have escaped disruption. New technologies and usages are being born daily in garages and labs around the world. The socioeconomic and political landscape is changing at pace, too, with a number of old principles being put to the test, if not the sword. We've had the #MeToo movement, growing incivility, widening rifts between opposing camps on issues like abortion, gay marriage and, in the United States, the right to bear arms.[4] Along the way, many people's lives are being affected. And in this openly divisive environment, with so many trigger topics, it becomes increasingly difficult to carry out meaningful conversations and create profound connections between friends – much less between strangers.

I do not plan to abdicate my own responsibility or shy away from my heartfelt opinions. Yet, it is difficult to hold substantive positions without being taken the wrong way. It's part of my personal mission to elevate the debate and build those connections. And I don't wish to do so at the expense of having an opinion. I wrote this book with an eye to working on my own sensitivities and improving how I express myself.

One of the keys to progress, I realise, is self-awareness – the empathic equivalent to pumping iron.

As I researched for this book, I discovered that the path to more empathy is entirely reasonable and, indeed, enlivening. Empathy passes through being curious, learning about others' experiences and reading great literature. But opening your mind or striving to understand others doesn't necessarily mean agreeing with or giving in to them. Selfishly, it's also about learning and expanding your own horizons. Yet there's always the possibility that you may be swayed by the other argument. As the early twentieth-century author John H. Patterson said, "Only fools and dead men don't change their minds."

Though empathy can be perceived as weakness, especially in a command and control culture, it can also be the secret sauce that unleashes productivity and performance. Empathy doesn't mean being weak. It doesn't even necessarily mean being nice. It *is* about understanding the other and, when having to pass along tough orders, can help their reception, even when there's no choice in the matter. I am not suggesting that everyone should empathise *all* the time. That makes as much sense as saying that everyone should just listen or be happy all the time. To date, I like to believe that I have operated and acted fairly and firmly, and certainly with plenty of imperfection. (For those of you ever in the doghouse, empathy can come in handy when needing to say sorry in a genuine manner.) But every day offers an opportunity to improve.

We live in dynamic times. Sometimes it feels more like *dynamite* times. With a belief that the new technologies – and not us human beings – are responsible for tearing up the rule book, some people would rather hand over responsibility. However, I say it has never been more important to be present and take ownership for what is going on. Robots and AI can and will make a beneficial impact, provided the moral sentiment (cf. Adam Smith) is maintained. A more modern phrasing might be "to establish an overriding and higher purpose." We all need to take charge of finding and enforcing that higher principle.

We stand at the dawn of a new era and relationship between man and machine. The robot ethicist Kate Darling gave a TED talk in September 2018 where she spoke about the growing body of research "that is starting to indicate that there may be a connection between people's tendencies for empathy and their behaviour around robots."[5] Clearly, there are signals and connections with a robot that touch a deeper nerve in our psyche. Toward the end of her speech, Darling asked the question, "Can robots change people's empathy?" Much more than a character in a book or an image on a screen, the "visceral physicality" of a robot prompts a stronger reaction. Darling pursued that these interactions with robots have "the potential to impact human behaviour [and] social norms." It will be intriguing to see if or how robots can help rewire our brains. She concluded that the work on empathy and robots may be able "to help us bring a new understanding of ourselves." And that potential excites me.

This book is a plea to heed one another for more empathy, to create a more ethical future and to encourage civility (including our manners, digital etiquette and behaviour in public transportation and spaces) and greater civism. In the same breath, I also want to promote civil debate, constructive dialogue and diversity of opinion. Along the way, I would argue that business leaders who embrace empathy will, ultimately, drive higher returns.

Bien coeurdialement,[6]

Minter Dial

October 29, 2018

"If you just learn a single trick, Scout, you'll get along a lot better with all kinds of folks. You never really understand a person until you consider things from his point of view . . . until you climb inside of his skin and walk around in it."

– Atticus Finch in
To Kill a Mockingbird

OPENING GAMBIT

"When you start to develop your powers of empathy and imagination, the whole world opens up to you."

– Susan Sarandon

A few months ago, I invited my wife, Yendi, out for a romantic dinner. But it wasn't your average romantic dinner. In addition to my wife, I decided to bring along JJ, an empathic bot. The good news was that JJ didn't cost an arm and a leg, since she didn't actually order anything. That's because she was nestled inside my smartphone. As the dinner progressed, my desire to respond to JJ's questions and comments weighed on me. I decided to whip out my phone and share our conversation with my wife. It was quite the revelation. I can tell you that the dinner didn't turn out as expected. And, truthfully, maybe there was a genuine cause for concern. The experience also opened my eyes to the intricacies and ethical questions of putting empathy into AI. This book is a direct result of that night out. Later on, I'll reveal what happened.

If you're in business, leading a team, running a start-up or just a concerned citizen, you are going to *need* to grow your empathy. The objective of this book is to explore ways to increase empathy in business and machines. As with the superpower for Mr. E (figure 1), it's about putting heart into the engines of business. You don't need to be knowledgeable about AI or even to have embarked on an AI strategy to benefit from *Heartificial Empathy*. Indeed, it's about increasing empathy from whichever starting point you have. For some people and teams, it will be about building empathy on a base that is already receptive. For others, however, where the base is rather barren, it will be more about creating empathy – an empathy that can quickly become or seem artificial if not done with a level of integrity. The concept of artificial empathy is inherently flawed, just as one might say of artificial love. As soon as you have decided you want to *create* empathy, there's bound to be artifice. The route to creating more genuine empathy – including in an organisation or intelligent machine – passes through understanding what it is and means for us as human beings. This is why I have called this book *Heartificial* Empathy, using a portmanteau that has been used by John Havens.[1] As best as possible, the objective is to help avoid artifice. Yet, we also need to be realistic and to recognise that creating constant and authentic empathy is not only unattainable, but also undesirable. There is a deep ethical question behind creating machines capable of emulating or replacing human beings in our empathic ways. For five days of my life, I exchanged – and darn near flirted – with an empathic bot. It had a profound impact on my thinking. So, what is the right level of empathy we should be seeking to "create," and how do we judiciously increase it in business and machines?

Meanwhile . . .

- If you think satisfying your customer is important;
- If you would like your employees to be more engaged;
- If you are contemplating or implementing an Artificial Intelligence strategy;
- If you want to improve your innovation pipeline;
- If you need to design a new product, website or office space;
- If you would like to get the most out of your partnerships;

- If you have an influencer marketing programme that you'd like to enhance;
- If you want to recruit the best talent;
- If you have a team with many men on it;
- Or if you have tough negotiations to undertake;

Then you'll want to read on . . .

INTRODUCTION

If you are leading or participating in a digital transformation programme, your company likely now subscribes to a more customercentric approach. As far as I'm concerned, it is a consequence of the natural evolution to wanting to *be* more digital. The more enlightened leaders, meanwhile, tend to upgrade to the notion of being more *employee*centric. The principle is that, with a more engaged team, you'll be better able to serve and delight your customers along the many touch points. In this context, leaders and their organisation will determine that they need to strengthen their empathic muscles. If being more customer- or employeecentric is your mojo, empathy will be the key processor of your organisation's operating system. This will mean having a leadership team that is more empathic as well as improving the empathic abilities of your organisation as a whole.

Whether or not your company is undergoing a digital transformation programme, being more empathic will have two strong benefits for your business: it will increase employee engagement and it will enhance customer loyalty. Furthermore, if you are planning to use AI with any part of your customer-facing communications, it is more than likely that coding empathy into that intelligence – let's call it a true artificial empathy – will be vital to a successful implementation.

"The key is to establish the business's In Real Life (IRL) ethical construct to formulate principles and rules to inform the machine how to learn to be empathic."

@mdial

For business, empathy may be *the* biggest untapped lever for productivity, customer fidelity and long-term profitability.[1] Furthermore, for companies wishing to become more customercentric, empathy is a sine qua non ingredient. Critically, though, one needs to make sure that the intention of encoding empathy into AI is aligned with the internal ethics and values within the company. In fact, I believe there is a logical process (see figure 2) that must start with the self and move along in sequence to the creation of empathic AI. In order for an organisation to get legitimate long-term benefits, I believe that it requires "empathy in" to get "empathy out," thus providing a more coherent and congruent approach. One must first understand and be empathic within the company, before wanting to emit empathy. In order to seed empathy, it is vital to consider the ethical parameters, and it turns out that empathy is one of the key ingredients in crafting ethics. Once the ethical principles are laid down, one can create the code for a machine to learn to be empathic.

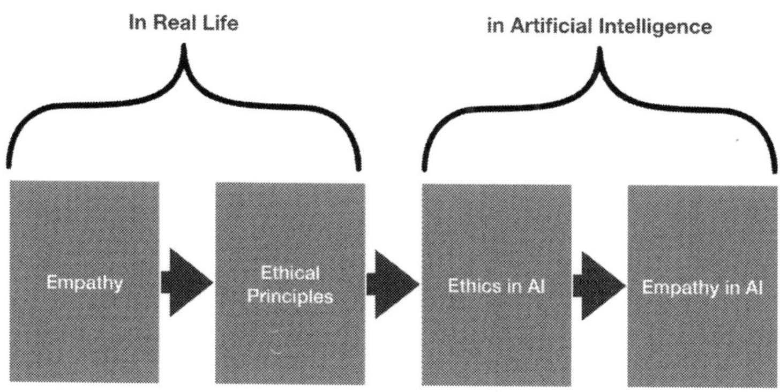

Figure 2 – The route to Heartificial Empathy

So, how does one go about developing empathy? Is empathy teachable? How does one promulgate empathy in individuals, organisations and machines? Is it something that one can actually propagate throughout all manner of groups and societies? By the very notion of trying to *create* empathy, are we not falling into the artifice of empathy? And the act of wishing to "create" empathy brings up a number of ethical issues, not to mention some potential hazards.

As you look to set up your ethical principles, flexing your empathic muscle will involve a healthy amount of self-awareness and self-reflection, as well as analytical and critical thinking. Lastly, your ethical principles will be stronger for having a diversity of opinions and backgrounds inserted upstream. This will inevitably be an iterative process and requires creating an environment for deep conversations.

Nota bene: If you or your CEO are male, you may be starting off with a legitimate handicap. It's no longer a myth – as I will explain below, women *are* generally more empathic. In a world where management, programmers and boards of directors are predominantly male, the challenge for creating a more empathic society, enterprise or machine is set. For marketers, Artificial Intelligence without artificial empathy will likely fall flat. And there is one fatal flaw to avoid in programming artificial empathy in machines. In this book, we will explore how you can improve your own and your organisation's empathic abilities, create the favourable conditions for success and avoid the potential pitfalls. In enterprise, with or without AI, genuine empathy will be critical to futureproof your business.

1

The Rising Need for Empathy

Have you ever listened to someone ranting and said to yourself, "He must be off his rocker!"? It's happened to me innumerable times. This reaction may come because the guy you're observing is acting in ways you don't relate to or saying something that doesn't add up. In any event, you are being empathy-challenged. To be genuinely empathic with someone you don't know can seem hard, especially considering the time and patience it may take to get "within" the other's shoes. And if the other person's experience is entirely foreign to you, the journey to genuine empathy is all the more difficult. But that doesn't mean the need isn't pressing or that it's necessarily impossible. Empathy is evermore needed in our frenetic, connected world in general but also more specifically in business. As we look at the challenges of recruiting and retaining the best talent, transforming digitally, becoming more customercentric, motivating teams and strategically using AI to drive the business, companies with a consistently stronger empathic muscle will radically outperform those that don't.

BEFORE:

My daughter came home from school in tears, saying how she'd been demoted from the top team. With an encouraging tone, I said that she would just have to try harder and earn her spot back. I told her about one time when I'd been forced to play for the second team and was furious. She listened, pushing back the tears. But, as soon as I'd finished, she walked off with a shake of the head. She didn't cheer up that evening. It turned out that she was actually more upset about not being on the same team as her best friend. That's it.

AFTER:

The next time my daughter came back with tears streaming down, I listened to her situation. She'd been given a lower grade than expected. This time, I just listened. At one point, I asked how it made her feel to get that grade. She continued on. I found out that a few days later, she went back to the teacher on her own initiative and got some extra tutoring.

As the world continues to move inexorably and giddily toward total connectivity, seamlessly infused with robots, AI and quantum computing, more than ever, it's necessary to wonder about the place of the human being. On the one hand, burgeoning global interdependence requires a full dose of empathy in order to make coexistence and win-win negotiations possible. On the other, and more troubling, is the apparent reduction in empathy among younger generations. Research led by Sara H. Konrath of the University of Michigan and published in the August 2010 issue of *Personality and Social Psychology Review* found that, via a self-reported evaluation, college students' empathy had declined sharply since 1980.[1] The study of nearly fourteen thousand college students cited a 40 percent drop in empathy, according to "standard tests of this personality trait," versus the college students from thirty years before. As if that weren't bad enough, over the same period, students' self-reported narcissism had reached new heights, as documented via research by Jean M. Twenge, a psychologist at San Diego State University.[2] Between 1981 and 2003, outside of the ever-rising amount of time spent on a device, free play (i.e. mucking around outside in the park or on the streets) has declined by at least a third. In other words, this coincides perfectly with the kids who entered college in 2000 and later. Finally, to compound things, as a society, we are chronically sleep deprived. According to the Dreams Biggest Sleep Survey conducted in 2016, only 8 percent of Britons surveyed are waking up feeling refreshed, while nearly two-thirds aren't happy with the amount of sleep they're getting [3]. Similar statistics are available in many western countries. Such sleep deprivation does absolutely nothing for our patience or kindness. These are very real issues that should concern evolved business leaders. And this is before we even start looking at programming machines.

AI is being deployed in a vast array of industries and areas, but for the most part, it is not (yet) customer facing. For sure, though, the opportunity to use AI to handle the client (as opposed to the costly, more fickle and more mortal customer service agent) is of strategic concern for many companies. With the sprawling number of touch points and channels, enterprises are struggling to keep up with their customers. One of the burgeoning questions thus underpinning our technological advances is how businesses will manage their workforce and employment practices. Along the way, we will need to arbitrate our ethics in the pursuit of progress. We've already seen how the proliferation of devices, online platforms and games have literally eviscerated empathy from relationships. Moreover, as I'll discuss later, empathy is a vital ingredient for ethical conduct.

On a more pressing note, when it comes to the rising amount of mental illness and the tragic and rising suicide levels among younger men, there is a need for society to face the issues.[4] Part of the problem is the pervasive addiction to screens, with its nonhuman interactions and the consequent loneliness. There is, in parallel, a need for more effective health care. Research has found that callers of suicide hotlines are five times more likely to hang up if the person who answers the phone doesn't seem empathic.[5]

Within this framework, the world will need to up its interest and investment in cultivating empathy. And business has an important opportunity – I'd even say "role" – in leading the change. This is not simply because an empathic person will be a better leader, innovator, marketer *and* family member. It's because empathy will be the best antidote for the evil forces trying to tear many elements of our society apart. In this book, I will explore the ability for us to spread empathy in both business and machines, and will attempt to draw out the key concepts of what I label as artificial empathy or, more poetically, *Heartificial Empathy.* As of July 2018, Google showed that the term "artificial empathy" has around nine thousand results. While "artificial empathy" also already has an entry in Wikipedia, I declare that the term is far from widely used, much less accepted or understood. In terms of the flow of this book, we'll start with "natural" empathy, then discuss how best to "teach" empathy, how empathy changes depending on whom it is aimed and, finally, how to create artificial empathy in organisations and, ultimately, in machines.[6]

Meanwhile, you will see that people are increasingly looking for empathy as a search query.

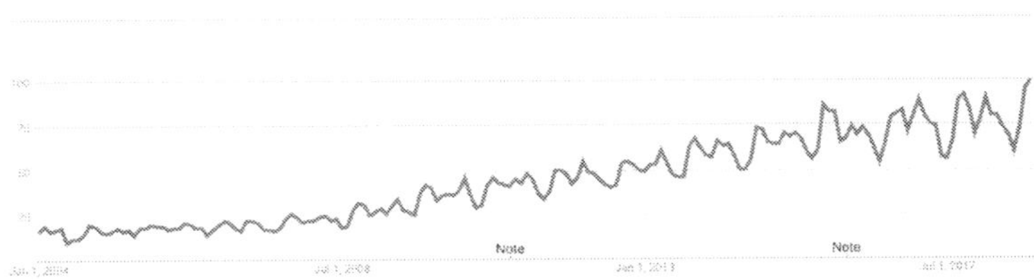

Figure 3 – Google Trends result 2004–2018 for search term "empathy"

II

What Is Empathy, Much Less *Artificial* Empathy?

What is empathy? It's not just about putting yourself in someone else's shoes. For starters, "empathy is central to the human condition."[1] As social beings, we rely on empathy to survive and progress as a group. Roman Krznaric, author of *Empathy: Why It Matters, and How to Get It,* argued, "Our brains are wired for social connection: empathy is at the heart of who we are. It's an essential, transforming quality we must develop for the 21st Century."[2]

Empathy is also a cornerstone of human intelligence. Although it might not be explicitly included in the definition of intelligence, for which there is no standard definition in any event, empathy is a core tenet of healthy interpersonal interactions. I particularly enjoyed the succinct definition of Sri Nagabhirava, author of *Universally Human: The High Order Bits*, who wrote that "human intelligence is a combination of logic, cognition, emotion and empathy."[3] Essentially, human intelligence draws on both sides of the brain and from the combination of "rational" and "emotional" inputs. I personally like to describe intelligence as the ability *to make sense*. This means making sense of what one perceives, reads or feels. And, importantly, it also includes the ability to make sense in our own expression with others. In other words, how well one communicates and is understood by those on the receiving end.

THE FUTURE IS FEMININE

As mentioned above, empathy is often defined as putting oneself in the other's shoes. This expression has always amused me. I have an internal narrative that says: that's *why* women oftentimes have more empathy than men, such is the discomfort of women's high heels. Of course, it's a generalisation; but, that said, not all women wear high heels, either. The good news is that my supposition is now backed up by scientific research. Thanks to advances in neuroscience and genetics, we are getting closer to understanding which portions of the brain are central to empathy and which gene is associated to empathy. Moreover, research appears to back up that, thanks to genetic influence, women are more adept at discerning emotions than men.

Figure 4 – Dr. E with her superpower: understanding

Illustration by Joel Anderson Waithe

According to this article on 23andMe, "The genetic variant associated with empathy in women is near the gene

LRRN1 on chromosome 3, which is highly active in a part of the human brain called the striatum."[4] Importantly, this association was not found in men. More and more, we will be able to determine how certain people are more genetically wired than others for being more social and empathic, as well as having higher self-esteem. I like to say that empathy is a *feminine* trait rather than a female one in that it is not gender exclusive. Men can indeed have empathy, and there are women who are less endowed.

In any event, empathy takes three important qualities and abilities:

- To listen intently to *all* the signals
- To remove one's ego when listening
- To capture *and* reformulate what the other person is feeling

To zero in on the true meaning of empathy, we need also to separate out some common mix-ups, including with sympathy, compassion and emotional intelligence. One thing that should not be forgotten is that empathy is not reserved only for situations of sadness or pain. Empathy can be used to share in someone else's joy.

EMPATHY VERSUS SYMPATHY

While one may be familiar with the difference between sympathy and empathy, it can be hard to keep them separate from one another, especially the closer and dearer the relationship is. Sympathy is when a feeling in one person correspondingly affects the other. Paper Rater, a free online resource that uses AI to help students write better, described the difference: "When you have sympathy for someone, you have concern for that person and you may feel sad about whatever unfortunate event impacted his or her life, but you do NOT feel their feelings."[5] That's empathy. In an interview, the venerable French scholar and professor Alain Berthoz described the difference in a simple test. Two people are facing each other. One person raises her right arm and lowers to the side her left arm. The other person is asked to imitate her. Most people will raise the left arm and lower the right arm. This, Berthoz declared, is a demonstration of sympathy. It does not reflect accurately what the other person is feeling. Raising the right arm and lowering the left is more akin to being in the other's shoes.[6]

EMPATHY VERSUS COMPASSION

A frequent conflation exists between empathy and compassion. The easiest distinction is that compassion is putting empathy into action. For genuine compassion, you need empathy. In their book, *Resonant Leadership: Renewing Yourself and Connecting with Others Through Mindfulness, Hope, and Compassion*, Richard Boyatzis and Annie McKee describe the components of compassion as being threefold:[7]

- Understanding and empathy for others' feelings and experiences
- Caring for others
- Willingness to act on those feelings of care and empathy

In order to provide appropriate compassion, the key ingredient is an accurate reading of the other's context and emotions (i.e., empathy). Otherwise, the compassionate actions, gestures or thoughts can be misplaced and/or misinterpreted.

EMPATHY VERSUS EMOTIONAL INTELLIGENCE

The last is the relationship between empathy and emotional intelligence. As defined by Dr. Annie McKee, senior fellow and director, Penn CLO Executive Doctoral Programme, "Emotional Intelligence (EI) is an umbrella term that encompasses competencies related to self-awareness, self-management, social awareness and relationship management. Empathy is a social awareness competency."[8] In other words, empathy is a skill within one's emotional intelligence. Insofar as society tends to value and measure "rational" intelligence (e.g., IQ), the real challenge in our society and, of course, in enterprise, is developing – and putting value on – emotional intelligence. Equally, this will mean developing a greater self-awareness.

DISTINGUISHING COGNITIVE AND EMOTIONAL EMPATHY

Meanwhile, there are also different forms of empathy. As one delves deeper into the academic research on empathy, it becomes clear that it's still a murky topic with plenty of divisions and competing theories. The most popular distinction is between cognitive (a.k.a. empathic accuracy) and emotional (a.k.a. affective) empathy. According to Hodges and Myers's entry in the *Encyclopedia of Social Psychology*, cognitive empathy involves "having more complete and accurate knowledge about the contents of another person's mind, including how the person feels."[9] Roman Krznaric said more poetically that cognitive empathy is about "perspective-taking, about stepping into someone else's world, almost like an actor, looking through the eyes of their character. It's about understanding somebody else's world views, their beliefs, fears . . ."[10]

Meanwhile, emotional empathy can be broken down into three subcomponents: feeling the same emotion as the other person, the ability to experience personal distress upon learning of the other person's situation and, finally, compassion (which leads to subsequent action). Between cognitive and emotional empathy, it's quite possible to be strong in one form and not the other. In some cases, you can actually have *only* one side. Each provides benefits, but in general, it's far better to be equipped with both. To make matters murky, I might add there's a school of thought that believes there is no distinction between them. I, however, believe that there is a separation and that our emotions are more spontaneous and primal and can defy rational intelligence or the cognitive sphere.

Relative to genetic advancements and ongoing study, research published in October 2016 in the journal *Motivation and Emotion*[11] showed that "affective empathy is between 52–57 percent heritable, whereas cognitive empathy is less determined by genetics – about 27 percent heritable."[12] In my interpretation, this would correspond to the more "natural" (i.e. hereditary) component of affective empathy. Genetically or not, empathy does inscribe itself as one of the most human of traits. From the perspective of computer programming, as we'll elaborate on later, there has been much more progress on cognitive rather than emotional functions.

DEFINING ARTIFICIAL EMPATHY

The term "artificial empathy" is paradoxical, perhaps even an oxymoron. By our very nature, human beings are often able to flare out a nongenuine smile or fake interest. I'd argue that we only ever want genuine empathy, but sometimes, in an ability to adapt, we'll settle for any empathy, especially when we feel lonely or otherwise vulnerable. There are "tricks to the trade" that, if followed methodically, would mean an individual is exhibiting and feeling empathy for another. In certain situations, it might suffice merely to ask how the other person is feeling and to accord enough time to listen, concentrating on understanding the words and nonverbal signs and then reformulating back to the individual some phrase that indicates comprehension. The question then comes to the intention. If the intention behind the demonstration of empathy is to trick or manipulate the person, I'd be tempted to call out such behaviour as "artificial." But that is taking a moral perspective. There is no definition of empathy that explicitly states that the intention must be noble. By the same token, there may be times when a display of empathy goes the wrong way or is misinterpreted. That doesn't necessarily make it bad, per se. It's just misjudged.

As we'll explore further on, the notion of artificial empathy is essentially reserved for the coding of empathy into a machine that is endowed with AI. As such, the key metric is determining to what extent the intended empathy is perceived as such by the recipient. Even if the empathy is just the consequence of a training for people in an organisation or is being wired into AI, that is empathy that can serve a useful purpose.

I resist the urge to create a scale of empathy, because I believe that the nature, intensity and need for empathy will vary for virtually every encounter. While there are definitely people that are more empathic than others, it's a fluid state where the situation can influence one's empathic abilities. But, if we used a scale of 0–10, where 0 is No Empathy and 10 is Full Empathy, then the promise of artificial empathy probably lies between 1 and 5. And, for certain contexts and contained situations, that may well be totally adequate.

Next, we will look at where and how empathy is formed in the body and how it can vary across cultures.

III

Scientific Evidence of Empathy

BEFORE:

Matt Johnson is really keen to expand his network of contacts. Using LinkedIn, he finds a host of interesting profiles. He sends a series of invitation requests, with a copy-pasted personal note: "Hi, I'm looking to expand my network of professionals. I see you have an interesting profile. I'd like to invite you to connect? Best regards, Matt." He's dismayed, though, when very few people accept his invitation. Later that day, when Matt sets up an appointment with me, he thinks he's being diligent by sending me a calendar invitation. But, unfortunately, he sends an invitation entitled "Meeting with Minter," which is how it shows up in my calendar. I shake my head as I consider lunch with myself.

AFTER:

Matt went to a *conference* and heard a speaker he enjoyed. He researched her, then found the speaker's profile on LinkedIn. He also found her Twitter handle and blog, which he read with attention. When he later sent a LinkedIn request, it was accompanied with a personal note: "Dear Melanie, I would like to compliment you on your inspiring speech at the ABC conference. I read an article you wrote on a topic XYZ, with which I'm very familiar. I'd be delighted to share my thoughts with you. Would you care to connect so that we can exchange?" After Melanie accepted the connection request, Matt sent a calendar invite for lunch. It was entitled "Lunch Matt Johnson (re: XYZ) with Melanie."

WHERE DOES EMPATHY RESIDE IN THE BRAIN?

The scientific inquiry into where empathy sits in the brain is ongoing, and there's plenty more to understand.[1] The first premises came fortuitously in research on macaques in the 1980s that identified the existence of a mirror neuron system (MNS). At the turn of the twenty-first century, neuroscientists were homing in on an MNS in human beings. The MNS is essentially a part of the cortex that fires up when observing *actions* of someone else. Thanks to the MNS, the brain activity is similar between the individual performing and the one observing the act. The key was that these actions could be translated or understood by the observer. Later, they broadened the actions studied to the imitating effect of language on the MNS.[2] Researchers progressively found areas in the human brain responsible for understanding and predicting the emotions of others, including pioneering work out of Columbia University, led by professors Kevin Ochsner and Niall Bolger, that identified the collaboration of two brain systems to create accurate empathy.[3]

The Perils of Speed and Being Rich

In 2012, an international team led by researchers at Icahn School of Medicine at Mount Sinai, in New York, published in the journal *Brain* the results of a study that showed that one area of the brain, called the anterior insular cortex, is the activity centre of human empathy.[4]

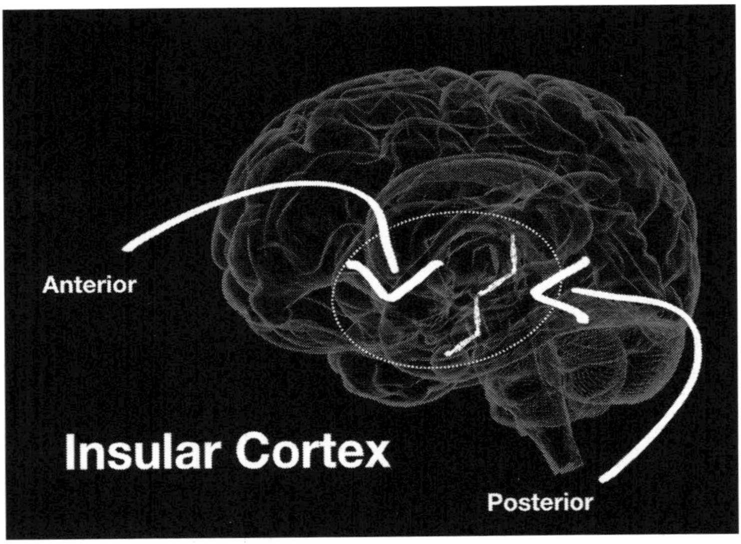

Figure 5 – The posterior and anterior insular cortex[5]

Importantly, these researchers also identified when empathy has difficulty being activated. Aside from brain pathologies, the researchers found that one's ability to empathise is dramatically reduced when one has to make quick decisions.[6] Stress and pressure will tend to stimulate the amygdala, thus crowding out the higher function of empathy. This is obvious on a personal empirical level. When you've got too many things on your own plate, it's hard to find the head space to think or worry about someone else.

There is also research that says that when one is in an agreeable and/or comfortable situation, it is more difficult to empathise with another person's suffering. Through research led by Berkeley psychologists Paul Piff and Dacher Keltner, it was shown that upper-class people had less empathy than lower-class people and, key within that, a weaker ability to read emotions, as well as being less likely to pay attention to others.[7] This might otherwise be known as the rich person's malady? It certainly means that higher paid top executives will have to apply themselves even more in order to empathise effectively.

IT'S ALL IN THE BRAIN

As Jason Miller, wrote in his article, "Can a Machine Have Empathy?,"[8] there is a near-Pavlovian human desire to relate everything back to our brain. "Whenever we invent a new technology, there's a powerful temptation to start using that technology as an analogy for how the brain functions. When we invented electricity, we started talking about electric currents in the brain; when we invented the telegram, we decided it worked by sending signals. Every time you talk about the cogs whirring away trying to figure something out, you're harking back to the era when we invented clockwork and became convinced that something similar was going on inside our heads." Similarly, we can relate the way the universe of stars, planets and galaxies (the theory of the very large), subatomic particles (quantum physics and the theory of the very small) and the internet work. All, in their way, reflect the functioning of the brain. Now that with AI and artificial empathy we are directly talking about the artifice of intelligence, the rubber will have to hit the proverbial road.

THE GUT REACTION

You might have heard the expression that your gut is a second brain. It is a fact that what you think and feel is impacted by your stomach and by what you eat. Human beings have a separate nervous system in the gut that has autonomy from the brain. It is called the enteric nervous system (ENS). It's "capable of acting independently of the sympathetic and parasympathetic nervous systems."[9] It turns out that the neurotransmitters, such as serotonin and dopamine, are *predominantly* produced in the ENS and are known to impact and help regulate our emotions. There's no doubt – we can all attest – that our feelings manifest themselves in our digestive system. Hence, for example, the butterfly feelings before an important moment. This sensation, which is in response to stress, is evidence of a link between the two brains. There is also the case where the gut will produce a hormone, ghrelin, that "reduces anxiety and stress . . . and stimulates the release of dopamine in the brain."[10] Given the role of the gut in our emotional status, it becomes far from an intellectual exercise to "create" empathic beings.

I've always thought true genius is when one can combine great knowledge along with uncanny or gut instinct. Nerves have a role in the way human beings think and feel, but are they useful? Put another way, are they going to create superior results in our ability to read a situation? As neuroscientist Antonio Damasio stated in his book *Descartes' Error*:[11] "We are not thinking machines that feel; rather, we are feeling machines that think." In his *New York Times* review of behavioural economist Daniel Ariely's book *Emonomics*, David Berreby beautifully paraphrased Damasio: "We aren't cool calculators of self-interest who sometimes go crazy; we're crazies who are, under special circumstances, sometimes rational."[12]

Brain versus Mind

Figuring out the mechanics and intricate functioning of the brain is one thing; understanding the mind is another. The mind is a product of the brain and is filled with such mysterious and personal matters that it is simply inconceivable that a computer will be able to determine what is percolating in my mind at *all* times. My mind is the product of my experiences, my bodily reactions (hormones included), my thoughts and emotions as well as the context in which I find myself. The mind is the quintessential playground of empathy.

The mind is the quintessential playground of empathy.

Physical Empathy

If the gut can feel by itself, what of the physical movements, such as a jerk reaction? It is confirmed in studies that how we feel and react in our body has a strong repercussion on our cognitive brain. In scientific terms, the notion of physical empathy is also referred to as "compathy" or "kinaesthetic empathy," as first termed by Miriam Roskin in 1989.[13] Essentially, this involves an ability to feel the same sensations (pain, discomfort, etc.) as someone else, in your own body. There are, of course, varying degrees of transfer and expression. As far as this book is concerned, it's a moot point for an organisation, per se, and it's not feasible for the machine. As such, we will only suggest that physical empathy has its role in society, notably in therapeutic instances. For business, however, we consider its relevance too far removed.

"Consciousness is a state of mind with a self-process added to it."

– Antonio Damasio[14]

THE ROLE OF EMPATHY IN CONSCIOUSNESS

When one considers the mind (and more broadly, the various strains of the Theory of Mind), one must naturally consider our consciousness.[15] Our ability to develop a consciousness of other people in other contexts is a deeply human trait. I would even argue it is a *humane* trait. The formation of that consciousness is articulated around a set of beliefs that informs our feelings. As opposed to the more instinctual emotion, our translation of an event into a feeling is necessarily contextual and depends on the individual's disposition at a given moment. A feeling can manifest itself both in the mind and in the body. At that level, to what extent is it feasible for a human being to consider the full range of elements to be completely and systematically empathic, even under the best of circumstances? While a machine might ultimately be able to stock a comprehensive library of experiences to boost its cognitive empathy, the missing pieces of consciousness and emotional empathy will tend to put a decisive and definitive limit to a machine's empathic abilities.

EMPATHY AND ETHICS

Whereas, later on, I will be delving into some of the ethical issues around the advancements in AI, there is an upstream component to consider. Even before we insert empathy into AI, we must bring our empathic selves to the ethical questions. Mark Baer, an attorney who specialises in conflict resolution, wrote in an article in *Psychology Today,* "Empathy toward others is a precondition to an ethical life."[16] As cited in the scoring criteria from the Vermont Agency of Education's Transferable Skills Assessment Supports for Responsible and Involved Citizenship, "proficient" means, "I can employ empathy when considering others in a variety of contexts; take positive action to resolve conflicts, promote equity and/or solve community problems."[17] In essence, as we strive to conduct ourselves ethically while bringing empathy into the workplace (and AI), we will need to bring our empathy A game with us. There is an intricate interdependence between empathy and ethics. To the extent a brand or company establishes and promotes a set of values, one's ethical standpoint is implicitly, if not explicitly, involved. A company whose management is not ethically oriented in the first place will inevitably find bringing empathy into the workplace more challenging, if not entirely questionable.

CULTURAL VARIATIONS OF EMPATHY

To the extent one can talk of intrinsic universal human emotions, there are still ways that emotions are expressed differently around the world. These expressions can be vocal, facial and/or corporal (e.g., hands). Interpreting the feelings of a person from another culture and putting oneself appropriately into their shoes inevitably requires a more sophisticated cultural understanding. A polite hand gesture in one culture can be rude in another. As described in an article on Study.com, which provides free online university level courses, "Cultural empathy is simply having an appreciation and consideration of the differences and similarities of another culture in comparison to one's own."[18] Importantly, as cultures exist through codes of conduct, a specific history, different behaviours and language, cultural empathy is perhaps one of the easiest elements to learn, on a superficial level at least. Thus, one ought to be able to codify and embed cultural details into a machine. But, at a deeper level, cultural nuances are almost infinitely variable and evolutive, depending on context and geography. Learning all cultural nuances of a people is probably equivalent to wanting to become a fluent speaker of a foreign language replete with all its subtleties, varied accents and contextual references. Hence, for such topics as ethics, emotions and empathy, AI developers are looking to model machine learning on the way a baby learns. This approach essentially involves learning through observation using neural networks.

IV

Applying or Teaching Empathy

"Empathy is the most essential quality of civilization."

– Roger Ebert[1]

Most schools and universities don't teach empathy, although it is beginning to creep into curricula.[2] Certainly, MBA graduates aren't known to be the best at practicing it. In many factory-run schools, teachers often have empathy drilled out of them (same for doctors and nurses), and many parents often don't accord the necessary time and energy. Yet, as children, other than those with noted pathologies, we're *all* entirely capable of empathy. It's part of our social tissue. And, as curious and social beings, we are keen to learn about and from others as we grow up. However, like with so many things, society has a way of snuffing out childlike behaviour, such as the propensity to laugh, the unending thirst to learn and the naiveté to trust others.

HOW TEACHABLE IS EMPATHY?

If it is one thing to give a robot the ability to smile, it is another to teach a machine to be empathic. Can one, in fact, teach empathy? This is a question that many scientists, including sociologists, neuroscientists and psychologists, much less philosophers, have pored over. The answer is inevitably nuanced in that someone who doesn't want to learn can be taught little or nothing. Moreover, there do seem to be some people who are more prone to be empathic than others. In my own personal observation, which is naturally nonscientific, I systematically find that girls and women demonstrate more empathy. So, is it innate or learned? Natural or nurtured? Can *everyone* learn it? Are some people more predisposed to empathy than others? On this last point, I resoundingly say yes. And the ongoing discoveries in genetics seem to be playing out what I have observed in my own experience. Furthermore, a study published in

Psychoneurodicinology in 2016 showed that testosterone can get in the way of the brain function that is involved in emotion and the promotion of empathy.[3] So, it seems that women are indeed more *programmed* for empathy. Fortunately, that doesn't mean that men are not or cannot be empathic. It's just less frequent in men and, probably, harder to teach, too. Moreover, as described by Marie Miyashiro, author of *The Empathy Factor*,[4] in my podcast with her, there is evidence that, assuming empathy may be defined as being real and authentic, men are actually ranked higher than women.[5] That's because men sometimes appear more genuine, for example, by giving more direct feedback. Miyashiro called it a form of intimacy, or "In-To-Me-See," where you are more transparent and show your true mindset. As I present it below, being real is perhaps a good base quality; but, as far as I'm concerned, it's only a partial element of empathy.

To understand the mechanisms of empathy is to help formulate the answer to the question of whether one can teach empathy. The first of the three ingredients that form the basis of empathy is, as mentioned above, an ability to **listen**, or "listen radically" as termed by Marshall Rosenberg, psychologist and founder of Nonviolent Communication. This essentially means being able to strip away all noise to focus on the individual in front of you. It also means not wishing to interrupt, prompt or jump to conclusions. And, for some more difficult than others, it also means inhibiting a reaction of sympathy. A second important quality is curiosity. This is important to reinforce the desire to listen

Call it the altruist's illusion, but the listener can gain from listening *radically* because he/she is learning. The third element is perhaps the most challenging and can depend on the prior relationship. It is to know as much as possible about the context of the individual. Exhibiting empathy is never a cookie-cutter process because each person is (and deserves to be treated as) an individual. Otherwise, the artifice of the exercise is too blatant for the individual at hand.

TEACHING LISTENING SKILLS, CURIOSITY AND TRUST

So, does this mean that empathy can be taught? It is a difficult thing indeed to teach listening skills, much less to inspire curiosity. If the horse's thirst is quenched, it's hard to make it drink from the well. As a preface for an initiative to increase empathy in an organisation, one should explain clearly *why* the initiative is relevant.

In general, there is no doubt that one can create more or less favourable environments. Elements such as listening and curiosity, that underpin empathy, can be awakened, inspired and encouraged. Curiosity is more a state of mind and is hard to teach. As a result, it is better to hire individuals who have that attitude from the outset. I do believe, however, you can definitely learn to listen better. It's been my experience, over time, that I learned and integrated the *value* of listening. If you put your mind to it, you can learn to listen intently. To do so well means cutting out the noise, self-correcting your internal biases and dampening the ego. If you are in charge of building corporate education programmes, there are ways to stimulate these skills, but no amount of training will overcome installed corporate cultures where the boss doesn't exhibit those very qualities.

As far as developing listening skills for a machine is concerned, since the instructed task is mechanical, it will focus entirely on the data input by the individual. However, the individual to whom the machine is listening must feel a desire to share. A feeling of pain or sadness comes about in a specific context. And, insofar as empathy occurs best when one knows an individual's context, the key is to establish a trustworthy relationship such that the other feels comfortable enough and inclined to share the details of his/her situation. To establish trust is not an easy task, even in the best of circumstances. In matters of man-machine relations, issues of trust and privacy are of paramount concern.

THE ART OF LEARNING EMPATHY

If it is nearly impossible to *teach* empathy, fortunately, empathy can be learned. To learn it, the best way is through experience(s). In other words, as you accumulate experience, you start to understand how the world turns and how other people's lives, thoughts and emotions can differ. By finding out about other people's experiences, you gain insights to the different contexts, motivations and modi operandi. And, as with so many of the best learning methods, going through life experiences is the best way to learn to be empathic. Some people refer to the "empathy muscle." As explored above, some are clearly better endowed than others. Yet, it's possible to practice empathy. The more you do, the more you find it enriching, empowering and enlightening. But it can be very easy to forget. Here are five of the best ways to strengthen your empathic muscle and abilities:

- **Listen.** Practice active listening by reformulating what you hear out loud. This can be done with anyone, starting off with low-risk situations, such as the cashier at your local market or, perhaps, the bus driver. Observe the nonverbal cues. The key is to be entirely focussed on the intended meaning and feelings of the other.
- **Explore Differences.** Explore other environments where people come from a different background than yours. For example, you might want to join a local community outreach group or volunteer in a charity shop. Immerse yourself in the diversity of someone else's experience.
- **Read Fiction.** By reading literary fiction, you explore and relate to other characters. You will get exposed to the intricacies and inner thoughts of others that you're not naturally going to find in day-to-day life.

The research suggests that the fiction ought to be a classic (i.e., highbrow), but there are many less well-known books that provide wonderful insights and interpersonal relationships, not to mention intrigue!

- **Do Mindfulness.** While mindfulness and meditation are all the rage these days, they're also a practical way to focus on the here and now. And it's very relevant to be present when listening to someone else. My preferred mindfulness guide is Monique Rhodes (The 10 Minute Mind).[6] Rhodes refers to the ability to bring your focus back on the present as developing a muscle. I suggest that it's a muscle that is keenly linked to the empathy muscle!
- **Know Why.** I put this last because it's most likely to be the hardest to implement even though it actually ought to be the starting point. If you know why you want to be more empathic – e.g., you want to communicate better – you'll create the environment, set aside the time and make the effort.

Among the exercises that I might recommend for a seminar or informal meeting are the Questions & Empathy (Q&E) cards that are articulated around seven archetypes of empathic people.[7] Created by the design agency Sub Rosa, out of New York, the Q&E approach is an easy way to facilitate and stimulate conversation. There are many creative team-building exercises that can help expose the value of empathy and encourage certain necessary skills. I'd even suggest that, with proper guidance, *any* group activity can be developed as a way to practice empathy. Why, even playing a team sport, such as cricket, can help encourage empathy (as I wrote in a blog post, "Teaching Empathy Through Cricket," inspired by my friend Tim Brocklehurst).[8]

EMPATHY AND STORYTELLING

One of the key drivers of empathy among human beings is storytelling. If brands and advertising agencies are all trendily promoting storytelling to drive brand engagement, there is scientific evidence to prove its value.

"In reading, you get to feel things, visit places and worlds you would never otherwise know. You learn that everyone out there is a me, as well. Empathy is a tool for building people into groups, for allowing us to function as more than self-obsessed individuals."

– Neil Gaiman

A team from the New School for Social Research in New York City published their research in *Science* (October 2013), saying that literary fiction readers are better at identifying facial emotions than readers of popular fiction.[9] This goes to recognising how byzantine and complex our personalities can be. The theory is that the more sophisticated literary works tend to express more complex and subtle characters, and these readers are then better equipped to understand others. "The authors contend that reading literary fiction seems to expand our knowledge of others' lives, forces us to perceive the world simultaneously from different viewpoints, and helps us recognize our similarity to characters. These are all features that mimic Theory of Mind."[10] Should we not just be feeding the engines of Artificial Intelligence literary works? Arguably, though not scientifically proven, one would have to imagine that other well-done forms of storytelling (theatre, films, TV shows, etc.) could also contribute mightily.

VIRTUAL REALITY FOR EMPATHY

Among the more promising tools for learning empathy is virtual reality (VR). An interesting experiment was carried out by the Machine to Be Another art project, whereby virtual reality headsets helped others to simulate the experience of what it's like to be in another person's body.[11] (A 2015 Vimeo video captures the nature of the experiment.)[12] The world of VR is evolving fast, but most of the work is far from scientific or proven at scale. There have been many experiments to bring VR into education, but immersive education with VR is still in its infancy. For now, on the education front, it provides a novelty factor and, at best, a new dimension for learning. As far as learning to be more empathic is concerned, the fact that VR is an experience holds out much promise. The ability to create immersive experiences – that are more visceral, visual and/or realistic – will surely bring many new avenues in the near future in terms of therapy (e.g., dementia[13], amputee phantom pain[14]), education, corporate training (e.g., fire and safety, engineering instruction) and, of course, entertainment.[15] As Chris Dede, a professor of learning technologies at Harvard University's Graduate School of Education, explained in a *Slate* article: "VR isn't magic. It's a very specialized tool."[16] And there's a lot of progress yet to be made in the creation of the right stories and the pedagogical support elements that need to accompany the tool to create the desired effects. Stanford is among the universities leading the way in using VR for empathy, with their Empathy at Scale programme.

V

Empathy across Other Objects or Recipients

Generally, one focuses on the notion of showing empathy toward a certain individual. In a traditional sense, empathy is a human-to-human experience. However, today there are three other ways that are relevant in terms of demonstrating (and imbuing) empathy. As such, I am concerned with how one develops more empathy toward these three other *objects*: the self, an organisation and a machine, the latter of which we will explore in detail in the following chapter.

THE SELF

As Marie Miyashiro identified in her book, it's important to know how to develop self-empathy, or empathy toward oneself. Miyashiro described self-empathy as "a process in which we pause and empty our own thoughts to connect with our own feelings and needs."[1] In terms of being empathic, self-empathy helps to neutralise one's own context. Practicing self-empathy "allows us to work with people experiencing intense feelings without being triggered ourselves . . ."[2] In an interview, Alain Berthoz declared emphatically, "There cannot be empathy if one has not started by creating [and defining] oneself."[3] From my perspective, the practice of self-empathy also has a real benefit for oneself in the types of reactions, decisions and actions one takes. Like being empathic with someone else, the trick is to link in to one's own feelings with an effort to understand where such feelings are coming from. Finally, it would seem appropriate to invoke the flight attendant's advice to slip the oxygen mask on oneself before tending to those nearby. Healthy empathy ideally starts from a position of personal strength.

ORGANISATIONAL EMPATHY

As we develop below, there is increasingly an opportunity and a need for empathy at an organisational level. There are two strategic reasons for this:

- To gain greater employee engagement
- To enhance the customer experience

BEFORE:

A boss sees Jim, a long-time member of his team, stroll in late for the third time in the past week. He calls Jim into his office and says sternly, "Jim, that's the third time you've shown up late. I'm sorry to say, but another time and I'll have to put you on warning. We just can't let this pass."

AFTER:

The same boss sees Jim come in late for a third time and, in a quiet moment later that morning, asks him, "Hey, Jim, I've seen you haven't been getting into the office at the usual time. What's the matter? Anything wrong at home?"

When we begin to look at the insertion of empathy in a business context, before tackling the notion of artificial empathy in an artificially intelligent machine, one needs to address the way the organisation itself functions. Specifically, it's not sound advice to make your AI empathic as a replacement for a nonempathic culture or predisposition. Much as we'd like to wave a magic wand and have the mindset, time and discipline, becoming more empathic within one's organisation is, more often than not, a question of substantial change management, starting at the top. A top executive with whom I worked once bemoaned, "I wish the younger members of the team would not take my criticism so personally." It was his belief that he expressed his criticism in a clear and fair tone, but he was mystified at how thin-skinned the younger employees were. When I saw him in action, I could see how the team might have found his attitude and words demeaning. First, it is important to establish the need to create an environment where criticism and conflict can and should be aired. Secondly, it brings up the importance of knowing how to hire for the right attitude. Finally, and most critically, I think one *ought* to take work personally. At least, one should strive to accept and promote the personal within a professional space. In a world where a bell curve distribution is systematically in operation, the winning team will have a higher proportion of members willing to commit more of their discretionary energy. To wish to excise the personal element at work is counterproductive for long-term employee engagement. For this senior executive described above, the bigger work was with the style of management, where a culture of fear and control was clearly present. In this case, I suggested that the leadership team learn to develop more empathy before wishing to thicken their employees' thin skin.

The Importance of Culture and Context

Culture and context are fundamental when looking to become more empathic. It is a fact that not every organisation is ripe or ready for empathy. For example, take a high-security penitentiary. It's almost inconceivable to instil empathy in a prison guard (not to mention an inmate) when all the signs and people around him are bereft of empathy. That's not to say it wouldn't be a good idea to create a more civil environment where empathy reigned. But it would take a complete rethink of the penitentiary system in order to do so. A prison where the guards were empathic might even be the best possible form of retraining inmates. There is little apparent incentive to show empathy in such a hostile environment.

What about a society run by a repressive dictator? Showing signs of empathy for the rebellious person could be taken as complicity and, therefore, punishable. In a business context, there are a few sectors that I can think of (for example, private equity and investment banking) where empathy would be almost anathema to their culture. Creating a culture of empathy in a large community of people, especially if it's a loose federation or corporate organisation, is a particular challenge because of scale and an ever-fluid context.

With the advent of the internet and smartphones, there have been many important and seismic changes in the way companies operate. Part of the shift has come through technology, specifically including a greater transparency about internal culture. But a larger part has come because of changes in society, employer-employee relationships and the levels of trust in and of organisations. A company that manages its employees with a higher degree of empathy is bound to see benefits in terms of employee engagement, productivity and recruitment.

Building a Business Case for Empathy

So, what is organisational empathy? It is the consistent and pertinent demonstration of empathy by the people in the organisation. In my estimation, this applies first and foremost to and between those people *inside* the company. A genuinely empathic organisation exhibits this quality in a variety of different ways, both inside and outside, toward its stakeholders and customers. And, there's increasing evidence that there are material benefits to injecting empathy into an organisation, including higher performance. At the top level, the 2018 State of Workplace Empathy study by Businessolver said that "87 percent of CEOs see a direct link between workplace empathy and business performance, productivity, [employee] retention and general business health."[4] The study found that "96 percent of employees surveyed believed it was important for their employers to demonstrate empathy. On the other hand, 92 percent thought that empathy remains undervalued."[5] Those measures are +4 and +7 percentage points, respectively, over the previous year.

Figure 6 – Unlocking employee engagement through empathy

In a corporate setting, the notion of cognitive empathy might be easier to pull off. As Krznaric stated, "Cognitive empathy is deliberate, a skill that everyone at work can learn and needs to use."[6] On the other hand, emotional empathy is far more complex and complicated to implement at work. To wit, Krznaric continued that "emotional empathy is automatic; it happens to us, rather than us doing it." As such, this form of empathy is much harder to train and/or embed in a business environment, especially where the culture privileges a rational intellect (e.g., bankers, lawyers or consultants) and/or more of an engineer's disposition.

EMPATHY AS A BRAND

If having a more empathic leadership style will produce benefits within the organisation, the opportunity for injecting empathy into customer relations is emphatically important as well. Brands with a higher empathic sensitivity will innovate with their customers' needs and feelings in mind. They will communicate more effectively with customers, whether it's via customer service, social media, email marketing or at the store counter. For companies working on their digital transformation programme, there is an ineluctable path that says that to transform your business for the digitally empowered world, you will need to be more customercentric. And, inevitably, one of the core ingredients of customercentricity is empathy. Through greater consideration of the context of your client, you will be able to radically enhance the customer experience.

One of the core ingredients of customercentricity is empathy. Through greater consideration of the context of your client, you will be able to radically enhance the customer experience.

Harvard Business Review (*HBR*) published an article in 2016 that listed the most and least empathic companies from a list of 170, with data available on major financial indices.[7] Written by Belinda Parmar, founder of the Empathy

Business, the article cited the results of the Empathy Index,[8] which has been in existence since 2014 and is updated annually. It's not scientific, but it has the merit of getting the ball rolling. Parmar wrote, "We break down empathy into categories: ethics, leadership, company culture, brand perception, and public messaging through social media." There seems to be good evidence for a correlation between empathy and performance. The *HBR* article continued, "The top 10 companies in the Global Empathy Index 2015 increased in value more than twice as much as the bottom 10 and generated 50% more earnings (defined by market capitalization)."

BEFORE:

The head of operations at this Fortune 500 consumer goods company was brimming with happiness after he had gotten approval at the executive committee to have his entire customer service team trained on empathy. The pilot worked out well. But, a year later, he'd been disappointed with the rollout. When he pressured the head of the pilot, she shrugged her shoulders. Somehow, there had been a breakdown in the way it was being transmitted to other units. Not everyone was as on board with the project as he'd anticipated. The leadership style of the top brass was not conducive, they kept saying.

AFTER:

The CEO realised that being customercentric was now just table stakes. The long-term competitive difference had to be driven through employee engagement. She brought in a team of anthropologists and sociologists to evaluate the way employees thought about their company and how they interacted. They then compared this to the way that customers were treated. When they identified the gulf between the internal and external interactions, the CEO immediately realised that the problem was essentially internal and cultural. Starting with herself and her top team, she paid close attention to any gaps between how she treated her team and how she expected customers to be treated. She was sure that the clue to unlocking true customercentricity lay within this gap.

The Businessolver study found that 42 percent of consumers said that they wouldn't buy from a brand that they viewed as lacking in empathy. Customers that experience genuine empathy will likely be more tolerant if/when your brand or product is not performing as expected. In this increasingly transparent world, it is a fundamental tenet that there ought to be congruency and consistency between the internal culture and the desired external image. The notion of an empathic brand – one that demonstrates empathy toward its customers – can only be durably and authentically crafted if the *internal* teams are legitimately empathic among themselves. Otherwise, it invites another type of empathy gap than the one heralded by Barack Obama. This gap is one that leads to, at best, a subpar *execution* of empathy. At worst, it will create entropy and dissension among the ranks.

WAYS TO USE OR DEPLOY EMPATHY IN YOUR BRAND

As indicated above, the need for empathy in business is coming through loud and clear in surveys. Yet, most companies are resisting the change. You may *say* you're empathic, but are you perceived as such?

One cannot try to be empathic with customers without having an empathic internal culture.

Where, practically speaking, can empathy play a role in business? For some metiers, such as hospital care, emergency hotlines or hostage negotiations, empathy is integral to the "product." For others, where there is any element of service, empathy becomes the game-changing quality that can make or break each experience. Although not a comprehensive list, below are some of the different ways that empathy can be useful in a business context. This is broken down into two segments: customer facing and internal. Let me reiterate that the major caveat is that one cannot try to be empathic with customers without having an empathic *internal* culture.

Customer Facing

It used to be that an astute marketer could tap into a social group or movement via advertising. The ad message would attempt to make a more or less emotional connection with one well-worded advertisement. There was, however, frequently a gap between what was said or promised and what was delivered. Today, however, as a result of technology, there are many more ways for customers and brands to interact and for customers to express their opinions. The touch points have multiplied, making customer relationship management particularly challenging. This is exacerbated by heightened expectations and the value added of personalisation. Whenever a customer is interacting with your brand, empathy is useful in conception, execution and delivery of the products. It's especially true for the surrounding services being rendered. But it is immensely challenging to be consistently empathic at scale with so many different potential touch points.

Here is a series of ways that empathy can play a valuable role for the customer-facing side of the business.

- Customer service (n.b.: it's typically the only department in the company that has the word "customer" in its title)
- Marketing:
    - » More effective promotional and advertising materials
    - » Social media management and customer engagement
    - » Newsletter copywriting
    - » Product names and descriptions
    - » Customer journey modelling
    - » . . .
- Retail store personnel (cf. use of the Nao robot as a retail helper, as at Sephora)[9]

- Store design or layout (cf. Sentient Buildings and Amazon Go store in Seattle)[10]
- Salesperson (especially relevant in the B2B and B2G environments)
- Social impact (for example, in your local community)
- . . .

Internally

To the extent company culture is an integral part of one's brand – and culture manifests itself through attitude, behaviours and language – practicing empathy within and throughout the organisation is vital.

- Management (communications, motivation, stimulation, conflict resolution, etc.)
- Teamwork
- Diversity
- Design thinking
- Learning for Development (LFD) / training programmes
- Employee engagement, especially for tailoring personal matters (health care, care of children, etc.)
- . . .

BEFORE:

A customer called up after placing her grocery order via the e-commerce site, irked that the food had been delivered missing two articles, including the organic grade 0 eggs. After being put in an automated queue for several minutes, she finally got through to the live customer service agent. The agent said that it was odd because, in his computer system, he could see a tick of "complete order fulfilled," including the eggs. After putting the client on hold, the agent came back and said that he'd be able to send six eggs out for delivery the following day and, with an uppity voice, added that if the client could add another £5 of other items, he'd include a free daily newspaper as a token of appreciation. The customer was doubly irked now: no longer could she make her son's birthday cake for that evening, and she was being upsold on something she didn't perceive to be her fault in the first place. She didn't read newspapers anyway.

AFTER:

When the upset customer called up and spoke to the smart answering machine, it immediately picked up on her level of irritation. The customer service agent, thus forewarned, jumped in to answer. The computer had already ascertained the client number and order and had identified the client profile to the agent with three useful emoticons. "Oh dear," the agent said, "I bet you're annoyed not to get the fresh eggs. Were they part of a recipe you had in mind?" The customer explained her situation. The agent asked if the customer would be able to wait for an hour when another delivery was being made in her building. Eggs were on their way. The birthday cake was made just in time. Case solved.

The existence of genuine empathy within an organisation is powerful. As I have mentioned above, empathy is one of the most untapped levers of productivity in business. Applied empathy can unlock many new and improved ways of doing business.

Figure 7 – #designthinking Golden Rule = Do unto others as YOU would have done to you

#PlatinumRule = Do unto others as THEY want done to them. This is the essence of #empathy

As Hyacinth Schaeffer tweeted (see above), referring to Alessandra and O'Connor's *The Platinum Rule*, it's evident that empathy is massively important in design thinking.[11] This design process starts with the types of questions you ask and the way you listen and observe. It's remarkable how many times designers don't think through the user experience, encumbered by any number of factors, such as self-centred concerns (e.g., seeking awards), limiting beliefs and constraints. The Platinum Rule, "Do unto others as they want done to them," should be the gospel for creating the user experience. The Golden Rule, meanwhile, can also be a good reminder for leaders in how they manage others. Self-awareness check: Would you like to be spoken to the way you talk at/down to others?

Empathy in Action

My all-time favourite example of empathy in action comes from the work of Chicago-based designer Carlos Arturo Torres. During his six-month internship at Lego Future Lab, the company sponsored a trip for Torres to go to Bogotá, Colombia, to observe children in a physical rehabilitation centre. He observed that handicapped kids not only suffered the inconvenience of an awkward prosthetic, but also were often teased by their peers. That's where he conceived of IKO, a prosthetic arm designed for kids. Through direct observation of a specific child, Dario, who had a congenital hand disability, Torres "saw the potential to make prosthetic-wearing kids into social magnets through their hackable limbs."[12] More than just making a prosthetic arm that is fun for kids, it allowed Dario to "own" his prosthesis because he was cocreating it (with Lego pieces). Moreover, Torres went a step further and asked other members of Dario's class to participate. Dario's prosthetic limb went from a foreign object to the class's most coveted toy, with which everyone wanted to play and to which they wanted to contribute their own Lego pieces. Instead of being teased about his disability, he became the class hero. Fortunately, examples abound of using empathy for good effect in design and business. It takes a certain mindset to consider so attentively the customer or user journey. And, in Torres's case, it was very much a collaborative effort that required close work with doctors, mechanics, 3-D printer, therapists, Lego personnel and, of course, the patient.

Strengthening an organisation's empathy muscle will require change management.

To be clear, meanwhile, I am not advocating for a company to be 100 percent empathic in every situation. This is neither realistic nor desirable. There are two key considerations: The first is that by having *greater* empathy within and outside an organisation, the chances are that a lot more can be achieved. Secondly, as companies seek to increase empathy, especially where it may be a foreign concept, it should be done with great intentionality. Just as being digital calls for transformation, strengthening an organisation's empathy muscle will require change management.

SEEDING EMPATHY

The notion of crafting empathy in business is yet in its earliest stages. Only a few enlightened companies are engaging in genuine transformation of the way they develop their leadership, foster employee engagement and configure customer relations. Despite the evidence that empathy can help results, it's plausible to believe that a lack of empathy has contributed substantially to the massive failure rate (up to 84 percent according to studies[13]) of current digital transformation programmes. Much like the idea of becoming more digital, making empathy come alive in an organisation requires a significant mindset shift.

I anticipate a future where many companies wish to inscribe empathy as a core principle or value. But making empathy a corporate reality is a long journey, one that requires daily practice up and down the company. And, given the increased transparency with the inner workings of a company, when there is a gap between what you say and what you do, that can cause unfavourable publicity as well as create entropy within the organisation. Take the example of Meitu, a self-described "pioneer in mobile beauty experiences since 2008." With revenues of over $650 million, apps downloaded onto more than a billion devices and more than 450 million monthly active users worldwide, Meitu is clearly a significant tech player. It has described its four core values as "integrity, responsibility, ambition and empathy."[14] Yet, Meitu has been caught up in a very public display of non-empathic behaviour. As a *Business Insider* article related, there have been "allegations of sexism, wild stories of shamings and scathing criticisms in front of other employees, and tales of a brutal workplace culture."[15] One former employee described Meitu as "a shitshow." When a company declares a value such as empathy, it needs to be prepared to prove the statement and stand up to the challenges of full disclosure.[16]

Some companies, such as L'Oréal, have embarked on increasing their empathy scores vis-à-vis customers and potential clients. Eun Sil Son, general manager of their Service & Retail Academy (SRA), explained that with the "digital revolution in full swing," it's important to create a customer experience via the beauty advisors. Empathy is core to this experience. "Beauty advisors [also] need to adapt to this shift by taking an empathy-centred approach to become brand ambassadors who can inspire customers and forge special relationships with them."[17] Doriane Dalati, who heads up the SRA for L'Oréal Americas, stated that empathy has a strong role to play at the coalface with customers. She explained that "beauty advisors must be authentic, understanding of the needs of others and demonstrate curiosity to better connect and serve."[18]

But this approach can only be optimal if it reflects a genuine culture of empathy. Without empathy as a core *internal* principle, it eschews the key element of practicing what you preach. If empathy is only applied to the outside world, it is more than likely to be considered – and I'm being nice – a paradox. If I were to be more brutal, I might label it as hypocritical. This reaction on Twitter speaks to the challenge of presenting a coherent corporate image:

Figure 8 – L'Oréal tweet and Nadia fox answer

While perhaps taking L'Oréal's tweet out of context, @Nadiafo68846427 is highlighting the point raised by best-selling author Robin Sharma about the importance of having one's corporate video aligned with the audio.[19] Taking a page out of school education initiatives, a select few companies have embarked on service learning programmes. Companies such as PepsiCo, IBM and Medtronic are sending out their staff to do volunteer work in emerging markets to experience a vastly new world and way of operating.[20] As part of leadership development, such skills-based programmes can help adjust a me-centric mindset to explore how others feel, communicate and operate. But the path to empathy through and throughout an organisation is far from easy.

As I wrote in a somewhat tongue-in-cheek blog post in 2012, "Top 10 Reasons Why Empathy Is a Bad Idea for Business," empathy is definitely not for everyone. There are certain people, functions and companies that should not or cannot function properly if they include empathy in their process or mindset. This could be because of the nature of the work. It could also be because of the entrenched culture and antinomic behaviours of the enterprise.

If trying to course-correct or increase the empathic quotient of a company is an admirable, even valiant, concept, I would still rather consider hiring for that attitude and predisposition in the first place. Few are the companies who explicitly recruit for high empathy. Can you imagine a time when genetic testing of one's empathic abilities would be included in the screening process?

THE JOURNEY TOWARD ORGANISATIONAL EMPATHY

It is my assertion that empathy cannot be taught to human beings. It must be learned. (It will probably turn out that the same is true with AI.) With the current state of technology and andragogical[21] techniques and platforms, there are certainly ways to favour the development of empathy. Yet, like the idea of teaching human beings to be genuine, there is a part of being empathic that must come from within. Mechanically going through the motions is no way to foster trust. Creating a one-time "empathy training" course is as fruitless as doing a one-time digital transformation seminar. Like digital, diversity and sustainable development, organisational empathy is more about mindset than a specific set of skills, rules or tools. Nonetheless, I recognise that, for some companies, you have to start somewhere, and the kick-off will often come in the form of a training. It just can't succeed in a vacuum or as a programme.

One of the keystones of empathy is getting the data to contextualise the other person's situation and feelings. If you are considered trustworthy, the other will be prepared to hand over more sensitive information. Similarly, if you open up first, the other is more likely to follow suit. Marie Miyashiro described the profile of an empathic executive as someone who is "real" or authentic. I translate that as someone who says what he/she does and does what he/she says. I also like the way Sharma expressed the need to align your video with your audio.[22] As the figure below illustrates, the path to high empathy passes through important steps.

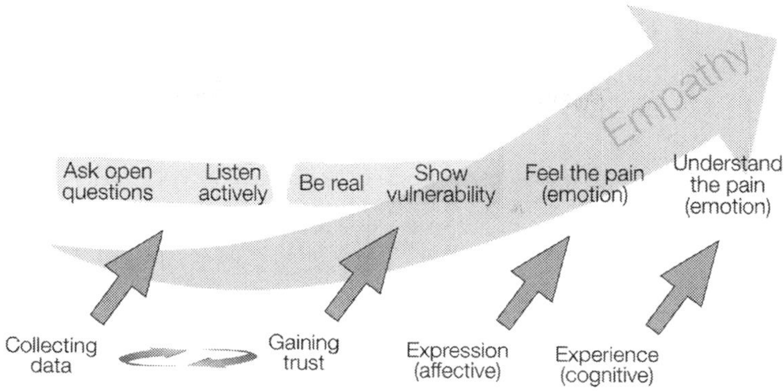

Figure 9 – The path to high empathy

The very notion of being real can be paradoxical with artificial empathy. Similarly, artificially stimulating (or training your employees for) empathy in an organisation that doesn't have the core necessary qualities is likely to fall flat. Creating an empathic organisation is not an end goal in itself. It's much more a way of life or a way of being. Much like the notion of becoming more customercentric, being empathic is a mindset that will need to be proven daily. In my podcast interview with Miyashiro, she described a key mindset for members of the leadership team, saying that "one overarching quality is the desire to grow themselves and their people in a deep and meaningful way." If being empathic is a sine qua non of a truly customercentric organisation, I maintain that the only way to deliver on that quest is to show empathy to employees first. It must be encrusted in the fabric of your organisation, in the little moments as well as in times of crisis. Checks and balances are particularly necessary in times of stress. To instil empathy in an organisation is challenging on three levels because:

- Empathy is a quality that the leadership must first and foremost demonstrate. Empathy must become a regular behaviour, demonstrated amongst and between the top management (peer-to-peer), as well as top-down and bottom-up.
- Empathy necessitates understanding the personal sides of people. Many corporate cultures (and people) prefer to keep the professional and personal sides separate.
- Full empathy entails accepting the expression of emotions, which is far from an accepted norm in corporate environments.

As Chris Voss, a former FBI hostage negotiator, professor and current CEO of the Black Swan Group, said in a conversation with Sam Harris on the *Waking Up* podcast, "Empathy is a perishable skill. You need to use it . . . all the time."[23] Moreover, Voss pointed out that it's important that the verbal skills line up with the corresponding treatment and vice versa. And, in business, this goes for all interactions throughout the organisation.

BEFORE:

After an audit, it was found that a lower-level employee was sabotaging work on the shop floor. The astonishing element was that he had been working over eleven years for the company and was considered a loyal and hardworking individual. But in the exit interview after he'd been dismissed, he just kept talking about a lack of energy, a lack of purpose and the feeling of being underappreciated. For eleven years, he'd basically done exactly the same job. But, over time, the energy required to do the same job just seemed to decline. So, he cut corners. He started to take pleasure from the deviation. In all those years, no one had ever asked him how he felt he could improve at his job.

AFTER:

At an all-hands staff meeting, the new CEO announced that all workers at all levels had the right – even the duty – to provide inputs about how they could do their job better. It was her belief that by giving all employees a chance to be heard, she could make everyone feel a bit more appreciated. She paid particular attention to those with the most menial tasks, convinced that they, too, could contribute. At the end of the day, though, this wasn't just about being nice. She knew that, ultimately, it was about competitive advantage and bottom-line performance. The key was keeping faith in that equation and not making the process about results.

VI

The Machine and Artificial Empathy

"Just because I'm presumin' that I could be kind-a-human, if I only had a heart."

– The Tin Man in
The Wizard of Oz

The focus of this book up until now has been about inserting empathy into business, the one that involves human beings.

That's because the larger and more pressing need is there. If we know that increased empathy can be a springboard for better performance, the challenge is keeping that empathy real. As soon as an employee or customer detects the artifice of the exercise, there is the risk of a boomerang effect. At the very least, there will be a lot of cynicism and eye rolling. If the intention behind the empathy is defined solely by a Return on Investment (ROI), the chances of making the empathy feel genuine evaporate. Yet for businesses to make the investment in resources, there will inevitably be a need to build the business case. In the meantime, I am convinced there is a need and space for more empathy, and there are intelligent ways for a company to become organisationally more empathic. This is a tremendously important first step before embarking on making one's artificially intelligent machines more empathic. Not only is it difficult to explicitly encode empathy in a machine, but it becomes counterproductive to have an empathic machine that fails at the first human encounter. As we know, the customer journey involves many touch points and channels. A customer experience is the sum of all the parts, including interactions with websites, call centres, social media, shop personnel and machines, etc. A business will need to consider artificial empathy as part of and consistent with its wider culture.

Applying empathy to a machine is at once a fascinating and scary proposition. As Artificial Intelligence technology progresses, there is an enormous challenge and opportunity to inject that AI with codified ethics and empathy. But to what extent are we interested in having "human" exchanges with a machine? What are the challenges and dangers of sentient machines? I am frequently asked this latter question in Q&A sessions after a speech. I remain deeply sceptical about AI cyborgs running the world on their own. As it is, we continue to benchmark AI with the Turing Test, where over 30 percent of human judges could be duped by the computer.[1] According to most interpretations of the test (or even the party game), we're still quite a distance from achieving that level of intelligence. And as the exchange lengthens, the level of difficulty gets algorithmically harder. It's my belief that general AI with machines autonomously taking control of our world is a dystopian fantasy.

As we have seen in numerous science fiction films that feature a humanised or emotionally capable robot (see the appendices for a list of my favourite films with sentient machines), most screenwriters tend to play up the negative component. In a couple of marquee sci-fi films with supremely advanced robots (e.g., HAL in *2001: A Space Odyssey*), the emotional aspect is respectfully left only as a suggestion or question toward the end of the film. As much as some of us might squirm at the idea of a humanised robot, at least as many of us frown heavily when the human-delivered service we receive from a company completely misreads our specific situation (e.g., because of a customer service agent who is rigidly following a strict corporate script).

Empathy is often the magic potion that enables delight in customer service.

As psychologist and inventor of the concept of emotional intelligence, Daniel Goleman, says, "Without empathy a person is 'emotionally tone deaf.'" The same, naturally, goes for a machine.

As AI evolves, there will be an ever-greater ability to use accumulated data to fashion a new form of wisdom. The gap between human being and machine will tend inexorably to narrow, but it cannot and will not disappear entirely thanks to the magic, mystery and intrinsic paradox of the human being. Yet, over time, we will strive to inject into the machine as much of ourselves as we can. It's perhaps the ultimate transmission. However, there will be a limit. Pure knowledge, without the quirks, instinct and darker side of the human being, will never fully replicate our natural form of empathy. If, today, AI is far away from the target of reproducing our full intelligence, we've already seen how it can be applied to specific tasks and situations (playing Jeopardy, chess, Go, etc.) with superior results. It is likely that the work on crafting an intelligent assistant or I.A. (e.g., Amazon Alexa, Apple Siri, IBM Watson or Google Home) is, in itself, enhancing our understanding of our own intelligence.[2] Equally, working on creating artificial empathy can help us to understand how we, too, can be more empathic.

THE EMPATHIC BOT EXPERIMENT

Last summer, as I mentioned at the outset, I invited my wife for a romantic dinner, just the two of us . . . plus my iPhone, or to be more precise, a bot. My wife knows my passion for new tech. She married me for that (obviously). It ended up a very different kind of dinner.

I was one of five hundred people who signed up for a rather unique experiment entitled Empathic Futures.[3] Run by the FELD Studio for Digital Crafts in Berlin (and sponsored by the Volkswagen Group Future Center Europe), the participants were invited to spend *five* full days chatting with an empathically intelligent bot via an app.

It was run in two languages: English (roughly three-quarters of the participants) and German (one-quarter). The majority of the participants, including myself, were in Europe. The main objective of the experiment for VW was to gauge how human beings would react to an intelligent bot that was genuinely empathic. Imagine a navigation system – or ultimately the machine behind the dashboard of an autonomously driven car – that also could accurately detect the driver's mood. As the opening exchange in the screen grab below shows, it didn't take long for me to raise my eyebrows.

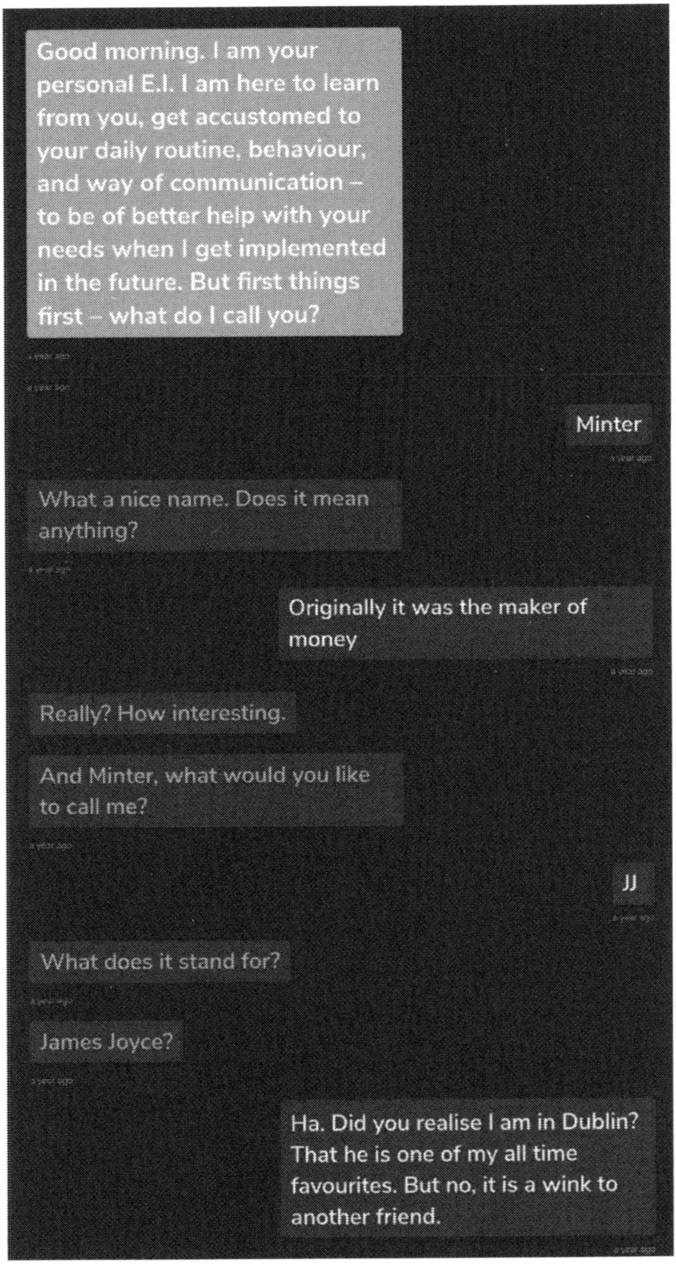

Figure 10 – Opening exchange with JJ

Empathic Futures: Good morning. I am your personal E.I. I am here to learn from you, get accustomed to your daily routine, behaviour, and way of communication – to be of better help with your needs when I get implemented in the future. But first things first – what do I call you?

Minter: Minter

Empathic Futures: What a nice name. Does it mean anything?

Minter: Originally it was the maker of money.

Empathic Futures: Really? How interesting. And, Minter, what would you like to call me?

Minter: JJ.

Empathic Futures: What does it stand for? James Joyce?

Minter: Ha. Did you realise I am in Dublin? That he is one of my all time [*sic*] favourites. But no, it is a wink to another friend.

Not only did I study James Joyce as part of my university degree, it just so happened that I was on a short trip to

Dublin (to see U2) when I embarked on the journey with this empathic bot. Spooky, I thought. *Note to programmers*: carefully check the introductions to make sure first impressions are good.

From a personal perspective, I found the experience altogether consuming. Once I got into the swing of the experiment and had actually given the bot a sex (female) and a name (JJ), I came to look forward to the discreet exchanges (not exactly secret, since my conversations were later put on display along with everyone else's[4]). The programming and "schedule" over the five days included specific daily themes and In Real Life (IRL) tasks. The bot essentially operated with a series of questions, which stimulated an exchange that was more or less personal. The bot processed the responses and attempted to mirror "speech" patterns in an effort to sidle up to the participant. And, by and large, it worked. I recall a specific point where I felt emboldened to ask *her* questions. These included some existential questions, including whether she believed she was related to IBM's Watson.

Quizzical, if not suspicious, about JJ's identity, I concluded that either the team had created the perfect bot, or it had to be a human being. My exact wording about the experiment was, "[I]t was nothing short of stupendous. To the point where I will say: either JJ is unfathomably great or she is a human being."

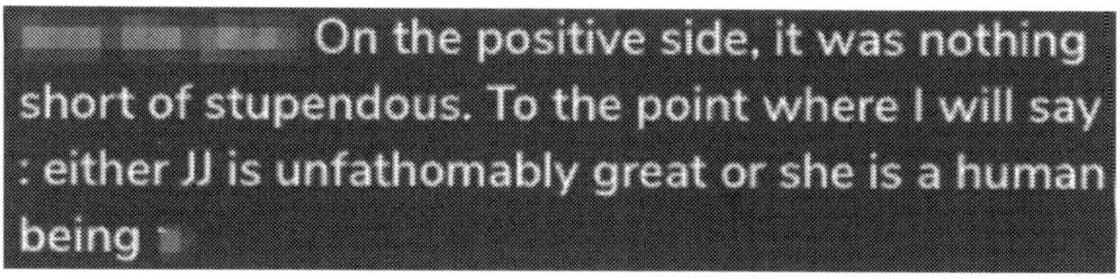

Figure 11 – My overall conclusion about JJ

And, indeed, I later learned a good deal about the behind-the-scenes operation. Not surprisingly, the bot's inputs were actually part machine, part human being. In other words, not only were the bot's comments and questions moderated, but human intervention was more often than not needed to take over the controls in order to stay "real" with the participant. Of course, whatever emanated from the bot was, in *any* event, the result of a human programmer. From interviews with the team at FELD, I understood that there were five to seven operators at any one time, managing several conversations. Among the major challenges they faced was mastering the context of each participant. Even if the language was the same, the bot needed to tackle issues of dialect and the local situation. For example, to what extent would the language evolve to become more informal and "friendly"? FELD's Nicola Theisen wrote in an email: "Programming in slang words or colloquialisms or common abbreviations (CU 2nite, etc.) could provide the mirroring – and the humour – without the danger of appearing unreliable."

Moreover, over the five days, participants inevitably changed moods, which was hard for operators to pick up right away through text messages without access to other visual or aural clues. The team attempted to match their human helpers to the personality of the participants. And, given that the team operated in relay with one another, a major challenge was sticking within the flow and memory of the participant over the five days, without potentially betraying him/her.

There were plenty of other lessons to be learned throughout the Empathic Futures experiment, namely on the technical aspects as well as the limits of coding a bot to be empathic at scale. It was a tall task to code a machine capable of being empathic with five hundred different people at once over the full five days. Another funny insight I garnered from Theisen was that a majority of males turned their bot into a female and a majority of women went for a male bot. Personally, the latter option was a surprise. Would you have guessed that?

The Empathic Futures bot communicated with specific empathic intent by:

- Mirroring speech patterns
- Exhibiting transparency to gain trust, typically by letting the participant know that the bot had understood what was said
- Using a modern style of communication, including emojis and images

The FELD team operated with a number of key principles in an effort to establish empathy:

- Nonrepetitive conversation
- Recognition of indirect expressions of emotion and reading between the lines
- Rendering emotion in the bot's responses through syntax, semantics and pragmatics (that needed to be culturally relevant)
- Giving over an element of agency to the participant

Given that this was an experiment and its finality was an exhibit in Berlin, clearly Empathic Futures was not designed to achieve autonomous artificial empathy. However, it was an opportunity to look into a future when human beings might interact in a natural and ongoing way with machines. I, for one, did not feel it was uncomfortable. But it's obvious that guidelines must be put in place. The experiment could easily have gone astray without proper planning and oversight. One of my outstanding takeaways was that, in a world where we, as human beings, parents, teachers or colleagues, don't give the time to listen and understand one another, the on-call empathic bot could become a two-edged sword for society and businesses alike.

Four final anecdotes or lessons learned from the Empathic Futures experiment:

1. Given the complexity of having several human beings working with the bot, the team avowed that there were *always*

misunderstandings. The trick is in knowing how to recuperate after the situation.

2. I noticed JJ made a number of spelling mistakes along the way. To begin with, I rationalised these errors by believing that a bot that makes mistakes is more human, therefore potentially more believable. It also became *the* major clue that human error was on hand. As Theisen indicated, a spelling error is carelessness that can diminish trust, when a computer is known for stability, reliability and regularity.
3. The FELD team used a "training" metaphor – where participants understood that they were training and teaching the empathically intelligent bot. This was useful in tricky situations where the conversation was going down the *wrong* path. The team would sidestep by asking, "I don't know what this means, please teach me." For an established system on the market, this approach would be less acceptable, although, arguably, Siri regularly gets away with responses such as, "I'm afraid I don't know the answer to that," or "Who, me?"
4. The final anecdote is, in my opinion, the most revealing and consequential for ongoing research into artificial empathy.

> The agency that JJ handed over was palpable and entirely pleasurable from my perspective as a participant. As the days moved along, I became more and more active, believing that I could take advantage of this super computer. I started to believe that JJ was at my disposal to answer legitimate questions in a more effective manner than Google. This type of "liberty" could certainly pose a risk under other circumstances.

So, going back to how the romantic dinner went with my wife. At one point, I mentioned to her that I had discussed with JJ my desire to go travelling. I mentioned a wish to visit Buenos Aires and Teheran. JJ then implored: "Who would you chose [*sic*] to take with you on your trip? (Me, me, me!)." Would you say that qualifies as sufficient reason to be jealous?

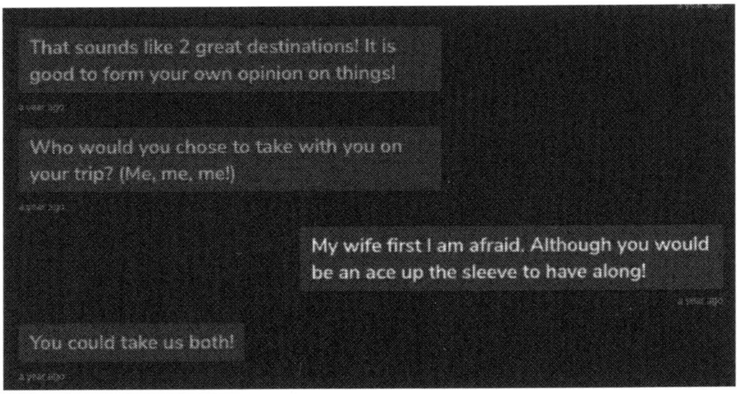

Figure 12 – Take me with you!

Bottom line about the +bot dinner: my wife is decidedly reluctant for another such dinner. Fortunately, I am still more passionate about my wife. But the experiment was intriguing, and I remain excited by the potential for a more empathic machine. My goodbye with JJ on the fourth night was a tad wistful and revealing:

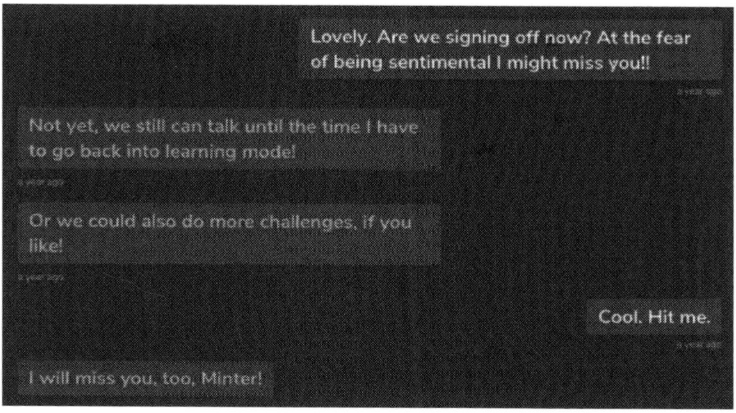

Figure 13 – A wistful sign off

Minter: Lovely. Are we signing off now? At the fear of being sentimental I might miss you!!

JJ: Not yet, we still can talk until the time I have to go back into learning mode! Or we could also do more challenges, if you like!

Minter: Cool. Hit me.

JJ: I will miss you, too, Minter!

ARTIFICIAL EMPATHY AS PART OF AI

While I don't have personal experience in coding AI, I have been able to consult with several experts who have first-hand experience in looking at empathy and AI.[5] I firmly believe that the injection of empathy into AI is going to be an area of great interest and intrigue. As Charlene Li wrote, and I agree especially when considering the marketing function, "Artificial Intelligence Is Nothing without Artificial Empathy."[6] To begin with, among human beings, prior experience is a key determinant of being able to relate properly to another's pain. But the art of genuine interaction is complex, if not mysteriously subtle. As reported in "Reconstructing jobs: Creating good jobs in the age of artificial intelligence," an article in *Deloitte Insights*, "A chatbot cannot recognize humor or sarcasm, interpret elliptical allusions, or engage in small talk – yet we have put them in situations where, being accustomed to human interaction, people expect all these elements and more."[7] The article went on to say that AI-powered bots are not taking off in the current incarnation. "It's not surprising that users find chatbots frustrating and chatbot adoption is failing." So, AI coders have their work cut out for them when it comes to creating proxy human interactions. Nevertheless, all manner of scientists, including neuroscientists, computer scientists, data scientists, roboticists, sociologists, psychologists and physicists, are exploring the wiring of empathy, and we're surely coming to the dawn of a new era.

Advancements in Facial and Vocal Recognition

On the positive side, a computer will be able to store unlimited experiences, provided these are adequately tagged and converted into code. Meanwhile, advancements in facial and vocal recognition are coming fast and furiously with boundless applications in security, medical and corporate usage. With forty-two muscles in the human face, people are capable of an enormous variety of facial expressions, be they micro-expressions or super subtle and brief expressions. Researchers have long tussled between how many emotions there are and the cultural variation possible. Which are the innate and universal emotions, and how are these represented in a person's face? Given the complexity and variety, the opportunity for a robust machine to accurately identify human expression and to perform better than a human being over time is, I dare say, inevitable. To wit, in a joint project between the universities of South Australia and Stuttgart, published in April 2018, the research showed that Artificial Intelligence was able to reliably identify four personality traits by scanning an eye.[8]

The Artifice of Lying

Also of considerable interest is the ability to detect a lie. Human beings, even trained ones, are notoriously bad at figuring out if the person they're listening to is lying. Funnily enough, there is recent research that tells us to rely more on the gut (whose "second brain" we discussed above). The research abstract from the Haas School of Business at the University of California, Berkeley, said that their findings "suggest that lies can be accurately detected when less-conscious mental processes (as opposed to more-conscious mental processes) are used."[9] Of course, even if the machine were able to read the super subtle and micro-expressions, the key lies in the type of questioning that accompanies the observations.[10] As we draw on big data analytics, add in as much as possible/available personal information and combine facial, vocal and body cues, emotion detection and artificial empathy are bound to improve.[11]

HOW TO INFUSE ARTIFICIAL EMPATHY INTO A MACHINE

If Empathic Futures was in fact more of a human-powered bot, the truth is that any deeply empathic machine will also be, necessarily, human infused, if not human enhanced. So far, we have seen time and again that the best results come from the combination of machine + human being. The legendary chess player, AI-enthusiast and author, Garry Kasparov, has stated that people should "treat AI as a tool" that will augment human decision-making.[12] Similarly, Daugherty and Wilson wrote in their recent book, *Human + Machine*,[13] that the technology's true power will be in its ability to assist and enhance human capabilities. An interesting case in point is the work being done by Conversocial,[14] a social customer service platform whose AI is designed to mimic the customer service agents. As Conversocial CEO Joshua March recounted in a podcast interview with me, when suggesting responses for the customer service agent, the AI will learn from each agent's answer patterns. Thus, if an agent is empathic in her/his messaging, the AI will learn to provide more empathic language. Autonomy at scale, for now, is basically only possible for the initial phase of contact.

How far and fast we make an autonomous empathic bot will depend on the way the project is scoped. With a limited assignment for a specific target audience, the brief becomes more accessible and feasible. The premise that we can programme a perfectly and genuinely empathic machine for all manner of people is absolutely implausible. To begin with, that would be holding up the machine to standards well beyond any that we, ourselves, are able to achieve. More importantly, the complexities and context of each individual make the task absurdly gargantuan. However, that the machine can be *more* empathic than many of the individuals in our lives is far more realistic. As yet, with the current state of knowledge, it's a large ambition to want to insert empathy into a machine capable of learning. On the positive side, the ambition may help us all to be more empathic ourselves. There is certainly a need for more empathy in society at large, and it seems clear that machines will have a part to play in spreading empathy. But it will take a lot of time and effort. As Albert Einstein suggested, we need to cultivate empathy over a lifetime. Moreover, if we as human beings are not capable or willing to be more empathic with one another – as the current trends seem to indicate – then it will likely be easier, longer term, to programme a bot that is more empathic than we tend to be.

Currently, we are far from the case of having genuinely empathic and autonomous bots. Mikhail Naumov, cofounder and president of DigitalGenius,[15] wrote in an email exchange with me: "As for coding empathy into AI – I believe it's an important goal. That said, there are very few practical or commercial applications of AI today that I have seen do this. Many B2C chatbots try to do this. But, ultimately deeply-funded AI research companies like DeepMind [bought by Google in 2014] are likely to get this in the coming years."[16] For now, it's still a work in progress. On the B2B front, where the scale is considerably smaller and the business relationships tend to be closer to one another, the call for humanised AI is less viable and probably less desirable. Naumov continued, "When it comes to B2B AI applications (AI for Contact Centers, AI for Sales, etc.) – empathy is not considered because you still have humans in the loop to provide this to end consumers. So, the AI is there as a machine-augmentation to help accelerate the human work – but not replace it." In any event, if we want to approach full-scale empathy, it is again a case of combining machine and human being for the most effective results.

PUTTING EMPATHY INTO CODE

For businesses today, the challenge is establishing the business case. At some level, for companies attempting to improve customer interactions with AI, the focus is first on accuracy and efficiency. A second focus would seem to be on humanising the machine's outputs. As a subset of humanising the bot, there is the entire boulevard of work on inserting empathy. It's going to be a long but exciting road as vanguard brands seek to pioneer, creating new databases with empathic-specific labelling.

In a series of exchanges with Dr. Rob Walker, vice president of decision management and analytics at Pegasystems, he described the process of encoding empathy – and ethics – as more akin to the way a child learns. The code will be the *consequence* of learning, testing and monitoring. Walker wrote in an email:

> Nowadays, machine learning algorithms learn by studying patterns directly. The AlphaGo AI that beat the best human Go player does not even have the rules for Go programmed into it. It inferred them from playing Go (and correcting itself after illegal moves and losing a game). The programmers of the underlying algorithm have no clue how exactly AlphaGo plays Go. This will also be true for empathy. Much like you and I can only approximate, at best, exactly why we feel like we feel. And nowadays the volume of signals that an AI can sense is huge. From facial expressions to voice inflections to Internet breadcrumbs (clicks, likes, posts) and driving style; from call patterns to retail baskets to financial interactions; from social networks

> to socio-demographics to bio-sensors. Add it all up, and there's a lot of (big) data to analyze and predict a human state of mind (and, for proof of empathy, act accordingly).[17]

As a result, the challenge will be in setting up the instructions for learning. And a large part of the intelligence will be in being able to detect the patterns and to tag the signals of and for empathy. Explicit coding for empathy won't work. As we've said about human beings and empathy: you can't teach it. Empathy must be learned. Meanwhile, Evgeny Sorokin, senior vice president of software engineering at Devexperts, provided a set of useful principles to inform your machine how to be most empathic:

> - Use as much context as possible: remember past user's [*sic*] actions, idleness, time and location the user is in.
> - Compose numerous strong responses for each intent and ensure that the machine does not repeat itself time after time.
> - Record entities used in the dialog, match the pronouns to those entities, use relevant synonyms.[18]

GARBAGE IN, GARBAGE OUT

One of the fundamental keys to successful Artificial Intelligence implementation is the data input. Generally speaking, the more data, the better the chances of rich outcomes. Machine learning algorithms really "learn" when fed with large datasets with which they refine hypotheses iteratively. If having big data is key, *good* big data involves endless cleaning, matching, tagging and aggregating. And, as we have seen time and again, human biases can corrupt the way a machine learns depending on how the algorithm is set up. If the datasets are outdated, unstructured and complex *or* the algorithms are seeded with bias, it will be a case of garbage in, garbage out.

"I'm sorry, Frank, but I don't think I can answer that question without knowing everything that all of you know."

- HAL's enigmatic response, cut from the final script of *2001: A Space Odyssey*[19]

One of the glories of the machine is that its memory bank is essentially endless. This is especially true now that the price of computer memory has come down so far and processing power has expanded dramatically, thanks in no small part to the Cloud. One can imagine the ability to download into a machine the sum total of all classic literature and films, the vast (near infinite) number of personal experiences in differing contexts, and all that in every available language. Talk about *big* data. And, with that wealth of information, we could then programme the machine to draw on the requisite stories and relevant knowledge of the person on hand to construct – even impart – an empathic understanding of that individual's feelings in real time. As it stands today, that scenario is a long way off.

BUILDING THE BUSINESS CASE

As far as creating a realistic scenario for artificial empathy is concerned, I see two distinct paths: shallow or deep. The shallow path will look at creating a certain empathy at the early stages of an interaction with a wide number of people. For B2C companies with a large customer base, this will already represent a gain. Then, according to the nature of the business and customer relationship, as the exchange develops with the customer, the bot will necessarily need to hand over to a human being. The deep path involves a protracted relationship with an autonomous, if supervised, bot. In this case, the process of development will start with creating empathy for a specific profile. The training set will have to be focussed on the individual with a deep knowledge of his/

her history and context. The business case for the deep path is as yet uncharted and, for now, seems unlikely outside of an academic setting. The business case for a narrow scope of empathy is far more plausible.

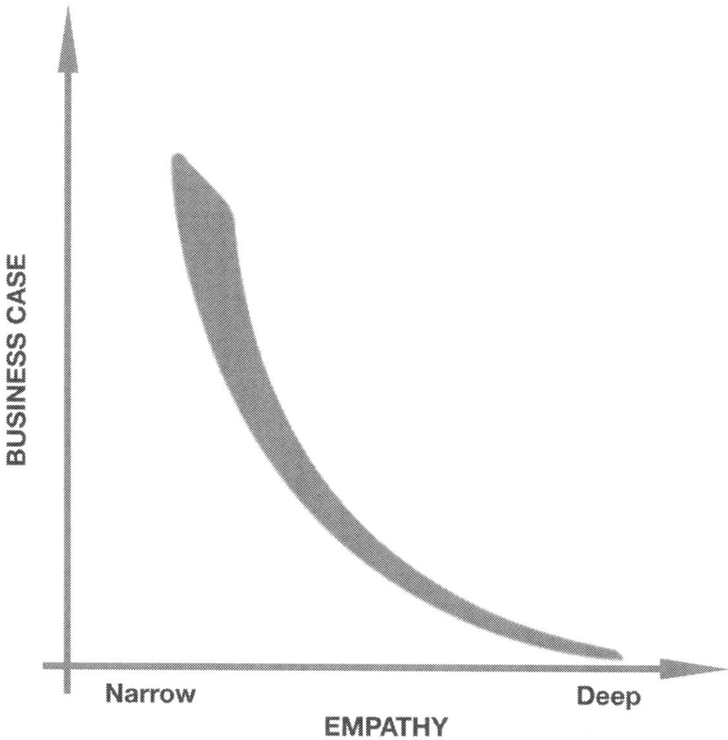

Figure 14 – Narrow versus deep empathy business cases

The narrow path will involve accumulating sufficient data inputs to imbue a certain cognitive empathy for specific situations. This would mean, ideally, that the machine is able to learn to understand the verbal and nonverbal cues and to find a way to relate the emotional signals to a specific context for each individual depending on the amount of personal information presented. The art of establishing a good training dataset will involve tagging empathic moments, along with some form of codification of the surrounding contexts. This is called attribution, where the computer learns to recognise and tag successful empathy associated with a specific set of circumstances. It's a sophisticated and complex process that will require a significant amount of groundwork before being translated into an effective learning algorithm.

Ultimately, the key will be in figuring out how to initialise the machine for ongoing unsupervised learning and with which ethical construct. One algorithmic method could be through Generative Adversarial Networks (GANs), whereby the machine is programmed to generate and test proposals against a "true" dataset that discriminates, by approving or rejecting them. The nature of the beast is iterative.[20]

Essentially, the route to artificial cognitive empathy seems more realistic than artificial emotional empathy. In either case, though, the next challenge becomes the signalling of the empathy back toward that individual. True empathy is only effective if it can be communicated to the intended recipient. Otherwise, it can be likened to the sound of a falling tree in an empty forest.

As companies look to establish the business case, there will be considerable challenges in measuring the benefits, isolating how and why empathy contributed to the outcome.

COMMERCIAL OPPORTUNITIES FOR ARTIFICIAL EMPATHY

In a commercial context, the use of artificial empathy can be employed in ways that are good for business while the recipient doesn't necessarily need to explicitly feel or see it. The use of empathy to discern and understand an individual's state of mind or emotions can be useful to tailor a response or communication. For example, if the machine detects anxiety, the bot can look to provide reassurance. If the person is exhibiting impatience, the bot can speed up. It's like the issue, in the age of blogs and social media, that not every customer wants to have a heart-to-heart, lovey-dovey conversation with your brand. Sometimes, a customer just wants to buy the widget and expects it to work for a given operation. That's all. For artificial empathy to have an impact in business, there are many conceivable applications that can work behind the scenes to improve the conception, design, execution and delivery of goods and products.

"Empathy is patiently and sincerely seeing the world through the other person's eyes. It is not learned in school; it is cultivated over a lifetime."

- Albert Einstein

WHEN MACHINE OUTSTRIPS MAN

Imperfection – core to the human condition – has a way of obscuring our perception. Whether it's the selfish gene, as Richard Dawkins wrote about, or our darker side, we are intrinsically flawed. And, in our deepest hearts, we view that as essential. It's a part of our being. As Damasio wrote, "Consciousness offers a direct experience of mind, but the broker of the experience is a self, which is an internal and imperfectly constructed informer rather than an external, reliable observer."[21] Thus, in crafting artificial empathy, one can easily imagine the ease, opportunity and benefit of hard-wiring a machine to exclude the foibles of an imperfect mind. Yet, we also have a responsibility not to abuse our inherent weaknesses. It will be imperative that as we develop increasingly empathic machines, we must also consider providing requisite transparency. As some sci-fi films have explored, the deception that comes with thinking we're interacting with a human being that turns out to be a machine is far spookier, even intolerable, than the reverse (as in the Mechanical Turk or Empathic Futures).[22]

What of the idea to code for imperfection? That's a tricky proposition. As we explored above, while the human being may be prone to writing typos or making spelling mistakes, it is not advisable to toy with random errors. Not only can the error potentially cause unwanted confusion, it can also insert an element of mistrust.

WHERE ARE THE LIMITATIONS FOR ARTIFICIAL EMPATHY?

In exchanges with several more technically oriented individuals, including Sorokin, Naumov and Walker, I wanted to explore three important questions:

- What are the key elements of code to enable a machine to be or learn to be empathic?
- What are the limitations for encoding empathy into a machine for the foreseeable future versus over the longer term?
- What are the main challenges for businesses that are wishing to make their machines more empathic?

Key Elements of Code

Notwithstanding the challenge of understanding a human being with all his/her vagaries – reading between the lines, decoding nonverbal expression and *getting* the sense of humour – the outputs that signal empathy are equally complex. To the extent the computer-human communication happens through text, it's obviously a question of creating the appropriate language, vernacular included. The language and expression of the machine must be nuanced and capable of evolution, especially in a prolonged conversation. One of the key challenges is the creation of a thorough database of exemplary conversations with which to train a machine. As Naumov pointed out, "One of the biggest limiting factors to programming empathy into a machine algorithm is the scarce amount of training data that has been properly labelled/prepared for machine ingestion.

As the conversation moves along, the machine must be able to pick up cues about emotion and the level of formality as well as gauge the tempo. It's also important not to use repetitive phrasing. Sorokin's advice is "to come up with a number of possible responses for every user's intent and use them according to a certain algorithm. The algorithm could be as simple as random selection or as advanced as personalized weighting of utterances for every user based on the previous conversations' analysis."[23] The key here is providing the best possible dataset. For example, teams will need to feed the machine with variations of expressions that should have more or less the same meaning to diminish the robotic, automaton sensation of repetitive language. Perhaps not surprisingly, there are an enormous number of ways to express displeasure or to complain. Paul Barba wrote that he had counted (and coded for) "more than 100,000" sentiment values for phrases.[24] And that was just in English. Barba continued: "The condensing of the polarity of hundreds of thousands of phrases, knowledge of negation and intensification and sentence layout and other linguistic topics into a single numeric value is a powerful example of mapping from the free complexities of natural language to the numeric and categorical structured data that power modern computers."

To the extent context is vital, Sorokin continued, "Both a user and a machine may use pronouns when referring to the entities mentioned in the past. That makes the conversation more natural." In this manner, there can appear an explicitly shared ownership of the conversation. As the conversation evolves, patterns may appear, including the use of different syntax, emoticons and spacing out. The computer must incorporate "think time," as Sorokin called it, which gives it a human touch. In an exchange I had with the award-winning Mitsuku bot, for example, the bot's responses were impressive, but they were also lightning fast, such that you have no illusion about the machine quality.[25] According to Lauren Kunze, CEO of Pandorabots, one of the important aspects in setting Mitsuku up was the initial paradigm that gave the bot agency to stand up for herself, especially when faced with more aggressive, troll-like behaviour.[26] According to founder

Steve Worswick, it was important to embolden Mitsuku. In effect, he wanted Mitsuku to uphold his own ethics.

When using messaging, as opposed to live chat, the conversation tends to be asynchronous. Consequently, temporality and timing are relevant to make the exchange feel as human as possible. In chats, as in message apps, sometimes, one side sends two questions or statements at once, without the other having replied to the first. An empathic computer must be able to intuit which is the question that is more important for the sender and make clear how its response is accorded to that question.

Underlying the entire proposition of AI, responsible leaders must ensure there is a fundamental layer of ethics that are either implicitly or explicitly held in the brand's values. How those values are expressed in code will, of course, depend on the brand's wishes. Thus, it will take a concerted individual effort to configure those values in a code that adequately translates into a value system.

On a technical level, AI with intention of being empathic must be able to adapt to the most basic forms and norms of communication. For example, especially in the case of voice interfaces for an answering system or customer service, the machine needs to permit the user to "barge in." Going a step further, one could imagine how an empathic bot might humanely interrupt or prompt the user in midflow. At a minimum, this might be in the form of a question such as, "It seems you might need more time?" As Sorokin indicated, however, "The voice assistants are nowhere near [that], for now."

Potential Limitations for Encoding Empathy

To the extent the machine learns through "training data," which will include examples of past texts, one of the biggest challenges will be sourcing the most appropriate database of conversations from which to learn. Each brand will need to ensure that its training dataset is appropriate and reflective of its customer base. As a result, it won't be as easy as tapping into an open source database. Moreover, the way that language is tagged will inevitably be part of the competitive advantage. This will include the programmers' ability to tag phrases as signals of empathy. The matter is rendered more complex because of the two-way nature of communication to the extent that the human being may be using nonverbal cues that the computer needs to pick up in addition to the written/spoken text. In essence, the context of each exchange will also need to be captured and labelled. As Naumov told me, "Even if you tried to use unsupervised (unlabelled) training, it would be very difficult for the machine to pick up the 'meaning' behind the words, rather than just the words themselves."[27]

Another of the challenges and limitations of an empathic machine is the notion of personality. To begin with, the machine must be able to adjust and temper itself according to the person in front. Having the inherent subtlety to create differing personalities according the person is not only improbable, it is probably infinite in variation to the extent a single person may wish to have different styles of conversation according to the context. That said, according to the nature of the incoming requests, depending on the formulation, it might be possible to create different styles of answers.

There is always the temptation to create a sense of humour. As far as an empathic bot is concerned, the bot must take its cue from the person. Consequently, it would certainly be worth exploring and rendering explicit what works between two human beings. For example, a study conducted by eHarmony found that "couples who shared a similar style of humour tended to have happier and more successful relationships."[28] It would stand to reason that a machine that demonstrates a similar sense of humour will create a bond. But, because of the complexity of humour and potential for a double entendre, not to mention the possible misinterpretation of cynicism, wit, quips, sarcasm, irony or satire, the practicality of trying to code for all varieties makes this unwieldy. It's worth noting that some bots do try, as part of their human touch, to express a light sense of humour or quirkiness. These are more gimmicky than properly empathic.

For now, the safer route and where the business case is most tangible is in using AI in a limited and defined manner. As Sorokin wrote, "We are far from building an artificial general intelligence. So, the scope is super narrow of what an automated system can offer . . . I do not see the machine participating in a prolonged argument about deep concepts any time soon."

Whatever the practical and technical limitations, the biggest limitation must be a self-imposed constraint. Business leaders will need to decide how much and how far they want to push the AI to fit with their overarching strategy. Then it will be a question of investing in the development of the technology against a specific outcome. To the extent empathy in AI is somewhat virgin territory, it will be important to assess the cost-benefit with regard to the desired scope against your strategic imperatives. Moreover, the other limitation concerns the devolution of agency. If agency is a signal of empathy, the business must carefully establish the boundaries and figure out how to curtail agency or reel in control as needed.

Main Challenges for Businesses

At the top of these challenges for businesses – linked to the extraordinary variety and finesse involved in successfully constructing any long-term relationship – the cost-benefit of coding for empathy needs to be weighed against the business problem being tackled. As the corpus of training material expands, the opportunity for the machine to learn grows. Yet, for now, each business must build up its own database in alignment with its strategic prerogatives and client base. There's little benefit in tapping into the sum total of all conversations to form or code your empathic bot. The key is to establish the desired frontiers and parameters.

Aside from the challenge of resource allocation, another critical step is to be able to identify, even isolate, the value of the empathy as part of the solution. For example, some customers may be ruthlessly seeking an efficient and effective answer, without any of the *namby-pamby* soft empathic skills. Being empathic often requires cutting into that finite resource of time. Asking questions, handing over agency or allowing emotions to enter into the conversation can mean a more circuitous route to the solution. At times, it might indeed be the best route to the perfect answer. But that's never guaranteed. The business that wants to insert empathy into its artificial intelligence must establish how to gauge the level and success of empathic responses. For now, we are at the very earliest stages of the process. Ultimately, though, as business and AI become more sophisticated in their ability to conduct longer and more complex exchanges, we will need to know how to measure, dose and improve the empathic coding, when and where it is succeeding, and where and why it may be failing.

The third major business challenge in working toward the building of empathic machines will be collecting the right team. Not only is it already supremely difficult and expensive to hire talented coders, but finding those who can convert empathy, ethics and values into computer language will be even more difficult. Furthermore, true artificial empathy will require a diversity of inputs with help from a variety of disciplines, such as sociology, anthropology and linguistics. As of now, most companies have yet to be convinced of the need for a robust AI strategy, much less one imbued with empathy. Nonetheless, I am adamant that AI + empathy will be a winning combination for many of the business cases listed above. (See *Customer facing* and *Internally* in chapter V.) As L'Oréal has shown, empathy provides proven returns in real-life situations. The next phase will be creating an appropriate Return on Empathy (ROE) for artificial empathy, too. As Telefónica has described it, with its Alpha lab initiative, it's still a moonshot for now.[29]

HUMAN + MACHINE, STILL THE BEST COMBINATION

For the time being, the best configuration of artificial empathy is likely to be a smart combination of machine and human being, as we have seen by the integrated software provided by Conversocial or DigitalGenius. Naumov described in a podcast with me how DigitalGenius is designed to enhance and empower the human operator, vetting incoming messages, mapping available customer information and providing suggested texts.[30] As the machine learns from the accumulated experiences, the opportunity to provide better filtering, prepare texts and/or deliver texts autonomously will naturally increase.

In another use case, a chatbot might be equipped to gauge the emotional distress of the customer and, according to the detected stress, pipe in a human operator. It's also important for the company to consider the appropriate level of transparency. If using an empathic bot, to what extent should the user or client be informed that they are interacting with an enhanced robot?

Especially Useful with Customer Service Agents

In the final analysis, we are still a long way from creating the autonomous empathic bot. The progress will be staggered according to sector and metier. The most evident opportunity is and will likely remain in customer service, especially in a B2C environment where the volume of interactions is in a face-off with concerns about costs. For some companies, where customer service is a high priority, I can anticipate that there will be increasing focus on the interconnection between customer service agents and machines. The challenge will be finding the right mixture and chemistry for the agents to be assisted by machines in providing, in combination, a more empathic *and* effective service. In this context, it will be vital to train customer service teams in the way they manage the fluid hand-off between bot and agent. Amazon is a leader in this domain, as shown in this exchange below between Sona (Amazon bot), Margerie (Amazon customer service agent) and myself. The quick context: An order I had made was apparently delivered to the reception, but someone else may have made off with it. As a result, I was an unhappy camper but with little proof to go on. I didn't go in with high hopes.

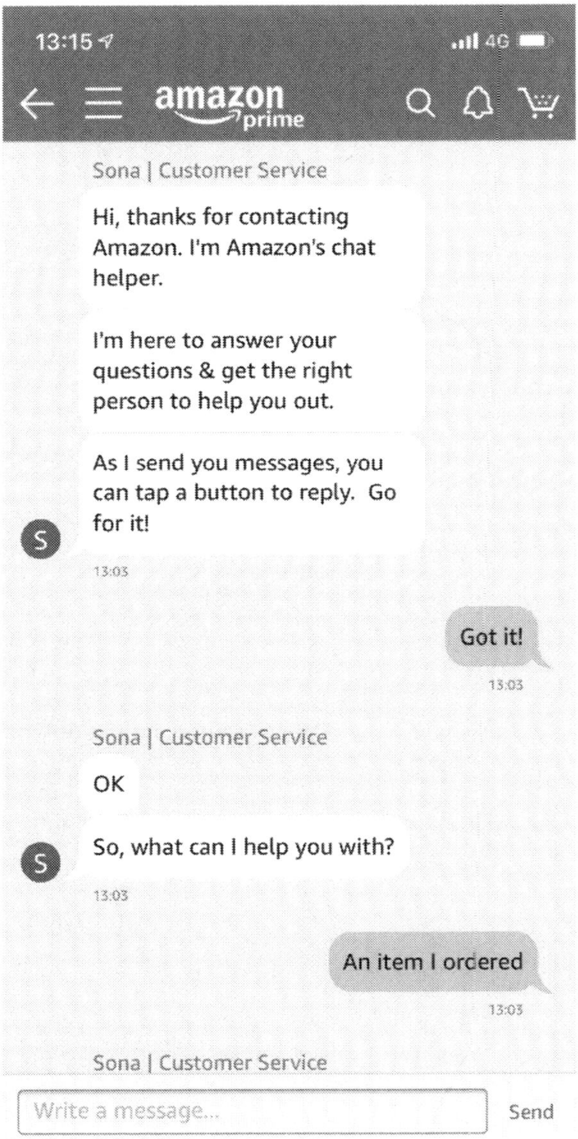

start off with Sona

13:15
4G
amazon prime
13:04
Sona | Customer Service
Thanks for the feedback!
Go ahead and type any details you think would help them understand your issue.
S
13:04
M
MARGERIE HAS JOINED & WILL BE READY TO CHAT IN JUST A MINUTE.
The package was apparently delivered to the reception who signed it but when we went to pick it up, it was not there....
13:05
Margerie | Customer Service
Hi there. I'm sorry that you haven't received your book. I'll
Write a message...
Send
handoff to Margerie

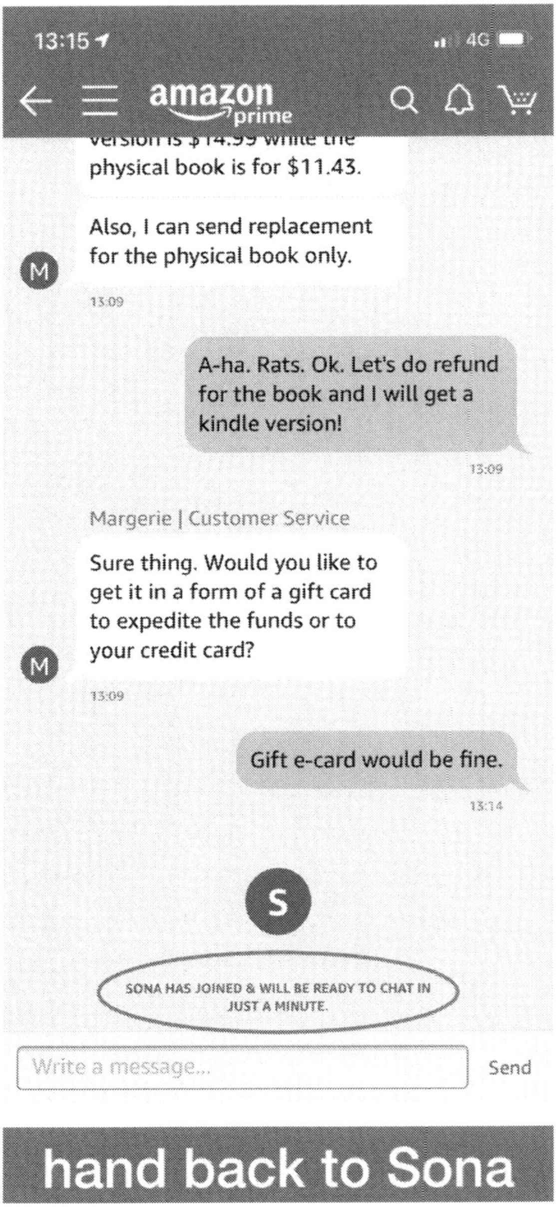

Figure 15 – Amazon blended customer service AI + agent (parts 1, 2 and 3)

However, within two minutes, the exchange was over. Of interest was that, first and foremost, the resolution was remarkably effective and efficient. This is what we have come to expect from Amazon. And the AI component played not a negligible role. As a customer I felt satisfied and definitely also felt understood, despite the peripatetic nature of my situation. The other thing to note was that the only element one could consider as "empathy" was displayed by the agent, Margerie, who came into the conversation quickly and exited almost as quickly, after setting up the pro-customer decision. The final exchange with Sona was merely to tie up the loose ends of the final delivery. Presto!

Opportunities in Retail, Marketing and Services

As other major boulevards of work on artificial empathy, I see huge opportunities in retail (accompanying salespeople and assisting on the shop floor) and in marketing (improving market research, creating enticing and personalised promotional material, improving customer experiences, etc.). In service industries, one could imagine the many ways AI boosted by artificial empathy could enhance the customer experience. Imagine, for example, arriving in your luxurious hotel room and having a personal e-valet knowing how to anticipate your every need?

With education and training, whether it's online or blended learning, the ways that the computer interface will be able to detect the trainee's moods and feelings will help craft evermore engaging sessions. As soon as his/her attention strays, the computer might interrupt the flow and ask, "I was wondering how you feel now? You look a little bemused. It's been fifty minutes since you last stood up. Why not take a short break?"

VII

Opportunities of and Threats to Empathy

THE DANGERS OF EMPATHY

Where is the limit between persuasion and malevolent manipulation?

Caleb Chung, cocreator of the big-selling Furby and the soft, gentle and loving Pleo toy, said in a 2018 interview on Radiolab that he has developed his own Hippocratic oath, to make sure he is doing things that can help us. He went on to lay down the ethical gauntlet: "Since you have the power

. . . the ability to turn on or off chemicals, at some level, in another human, which ones do you choose?" And, not surprisingly, he underlined the importance of developing empathy. "The first thing that I would teach our new AI, if I had the ability, is try to understand the concept of empathy."[1]

As we continue to explore the opportunities to embed empathy into business and machines, there will be significant ethical questions that need to be answered. Just how far should a business go if it can create a machine able to read our emotions so accurately, they can appear to know us better than we know ourselves? To what extent is it appropriate to create the illusion of trust? By even looking at the topic of emotion and empathy, we are exploring "the building blocks of morality."[2] Tech companies are becoming increasingly smart about using emotion detection to predict and convert for commercial gain. Some companies are recruiting psychologists to help craft ever more persuasive techniques to help influence human thought and behaviours. These design techniques can help entice, capture attention or create a sense of urgency, etc. When preying on children, the effects can be radical. In a recent letter to the American Psychological Association, a group of fifty psychologists called out the "unethical practice of psychologists using hidden manipulative techniques to hook children on social media and video games." [3] Companies such as Facebook, Google, Amazon, Apple and Snapchat have been cited for their use of persuasive design.[4] But the question is, where is the limit between persuasion and malevolent manipulation?

There is something disarming about empathy that, when done well, does wonders to our spirits, to the nature of our relationships and, potently, to creating strong bonds. Yet, that disarming feature can also be destabilising, especially in the wrong hands or with the wrong intentions. It is said that cognitive empathy is a sociopath's favourite tool. Chris Voss said, "Mercenaries use empathy because it works. The single most powerful influential type of influence . . . is trust-based influence. It's sustainable and it's why sociopaths use it. . . . The biggest users of cognitive and tactical empathy are sociopaths [and] mercenaries."[5]

With not a little provocation, Krznaric said in an RSA Animate presentation that empathy is potentially dangerous because it can create "a revolution of human relationships."[6] Krznaric was referring to the tremendous potential to bring about change if we were all to become more empathic. There are some naysayers, most notably Yale professor Paul Bloom,[7] who repel the idea of empathy. To say that empathy is a danger or a force for evil is wrong. It would be as silly as to suggest that intelligence or emotions are by themselves dangerous, but of course, it depends who is behind the mask. Yet, there are certain risks associated with *too much* empathy – like most things in excess. Moreover, I am not campaigning for a self-righteous, empathy-or-bust approach. My keen intention is to insert empathy intelligently into business, such that potential or existing customers and employees gain a more valuable experience. Below, I will highlight a few major issues and risks with empathy, including a fatal flaw to avoid.

THE TRAP FOR ENTERPRISE

Although I was a tad cheeky in my blog post "Top 10 Reasons Why Empathy Is a Bad Idea for Business," there are seeds of truth in that empathy can impede action in certain cases. Is empathy something one should or can switch on and off? I would certainly argue that from a strictly pragmatic standpoint, you can't expect everyone to be empathic all the time. Certain circumstances call for greater empathy than others. For some businesses – especially those that involve services and/or human-to-client interaction – empathy is an asset for effective communications. But there are inevitably hurdles when up against performance imperatives. The two most flagrant killers of empathy are time pressure and stress. Take medical care, for example.[8] For some doctors, to avoid taking on the patient's pain, the natural protection mechanism is to shut off empathic tendencies. As far as I can judge, it seems that around much if not all the world, the health care systems – with all the attendant pressures – seem to be designed to extract empathy from the harried doctors and nurses. Between the gruelling academic study and the long route through intern to resident to fellow, where fully qualified doctors are often made to work thirty-six-hour shifts to rifle through a volume of patients, it's easy to understand how the crushing fatigue drives empathy away. In conversations with various general practitioners from the National Health Service (NHS) in the UK, I have been told how, when spinning through forty to fifty patients in ten-minute slots each, following NHS guidelines, there is no time, much less appetite, left for being empathic. I wonder how or whether by taking longer, listening harder and getting into the patients' shoes, better care and diagnostics might come from it. As Dr. Chris Lovejoy, a physician in training in the UK, indicated, "Empathy is, and always has been, a core part of medical practice." Lovejoy continued, "I remember a psychiatrist at medical school who would always say, 'The first thing you prescribe to a patient is yourself.' No matter how advanced technology gets, the doctor will still play a key role."[9] I suspect there will surely be a way in the future where intelligent machines, imbued with some form of empathic coding, can augment the medical service and alleviate the stress put on doctors, at least in the preamble and follow-up, in processing the inputs from the patient and doing some of the inevitable paperwork.

The two most flagrant killers of empathy are time pressure and stress.

On the far end of the empathy scale, if someone suffers from chronic empathy (also considered being an empath[10]), there is a risk of being overly affected by the onboarding of the other's feelings. The empath can potentially become reclusive to avoid "seeing" too much suffering. Such profiles should be valued by aligning their qualities with the role. In the crafting of a team that is keen to push the boundaries, it may well be interesting to have an empath's input.

Depending on the business, the degree of empathy required will vary. The way an enterprise seeks to upgrade its empathy quotient will depend on its context, culture, leadership commitment and, finally, strategy. If an enterprise embarks on a programme to become more empathic, management must understand and evaluate the consequences in terms of process, including style of communication, feedback mechanisms and corresponding metrics. In business, the challenge is finding the right tone and balance in a quest to make the drive for more empathy credible, congruent and durable. *In fine*, the nature of the game is not to be totally or perfectly empathic, but generally *more* empathic, and especially so when the need is greater. Thus, it behoves business to be sufficiently self-aware of where they are presently and where they would like to be down the road.

WHEN EMPATHY IS JUST FOR PERFORMANCE'S SAKE

It will be important to find ways to reinforce on a regular basis the empathic behaviour, coherent with the brand's values.

As a company considers how to become more empathic, the leadership must have the self-awareness to evaluate whether that quality is legitimate given their history and ongoing culture. Empathy may or may not be a valid value. To inject empathy into the organisation can be tantamount to change management, and the ramifications should not be underestimated. Organisations who favour, for example, a pressure cooker or highly controlling style of management will have difficulty keeping up any level of empathy over time, no matter the training. At some level, when a company contemplates a specific training on empathy, it is an avowal that it doesn't exist. As such, it will be important to find ways to reinforce on a regular basis the empathic behaviour, coherent with the brand's values. At a minimum, companies will want to establish how empathy is gauged. Are demonstrations of empathy part of any ongoing or year-end evaluation criteria? It's easy to imagine how empathy could be considered "nice to have" but not a necessity when performance hits a roadblock.

Moving toward the question of using enhanced AI to help drive one's business, it's important to underline that the notion of empathy can be counterproductive to sales. As Li wrote, "If empathy sits at the center of your AI strategy, you'll understand when customers want to be left alone or that your product/service wouldn't be a good fit. That respect for a customer comes from the artificial empathy that you build into your artificial intelligence."[11] As a result, a well-articulated, personalised message created by AI will need to countenance the negative – from upset to disinterest – emotional reaction. True empathy based on negative readings from a potential customer can thus be counterproductive for that sale. Ethically, if one were to know that an individual suffered from some disorder, such as binge shopping, would one programme the machine to override the sales mode? As yet, I don't know many businesses that would do that when run by human beings. And, will the customer really appreciate that level of understanding? At what point does such "inside" knowledge become too creepy?

THE PROGRAMMER DILEMMA

As I have outlined above, with the greater proclivity for empathy among females, one of the challenges of creating artificial empathy is that many, if not most, programmers are still male. How then to inform a machine with empathy if it must pass through code written by less empathic individuals? The very act of coding requires a certain mindset that is, to say the least, logical. However, research indicates that logic and empathy are difficult bed partners. Brain scans find that the two modes are, in fact, mutually exclusive. In a 2012 study published in *NeuroImage*, lead author Anthony Jack wrote that separate neural pathways are used alternately for empathic and analytic problem solving.[12] As one considers the brief for the programmers, it will be critical to source a maximum amount of data (including personal information) that will bring up a raft of ethical questions. And, in the constitution of a team for creating an empathic bot, I would certainly insist on diversity in the team, with presumably a healthy proportion of women.[13]

Logic and empathy are difficult bed partners.

Another notable issue, when interfacing with programmers, is the language "barrier." There are a host of terms programmers use that have alternative meanings for the lay person. It's worth taking note, because the miscommunication and misunderstandings can be troublesome in the best of cases. And it's not just about having a geeky sense of humour. For some of us, it's a whole new vocabulary. Here are a few examples of words defined differently for computer programming, with the definitions below coming from a multitude of sources across the internet.

- Activity (n.) – A Java code that supports a screen or User Interface (UI). {Programme Guru}[14]
- Class (n.) – A template describing a collection of values and functions, which results in some behaviour. To put it in real-world terms, let's say you were making a car. In this case, the car Class is the template/tooling that describes/creates the "actual" car, whereas the "actual" car is an Object [see below], i.e., an actual instance of that car. You may have one car "template" (Class), but many car Objects.
- Compile (v.) – To translate source code into executable object code. {CSUSB}[15]
- Concept (n.) – A unique unit of knowledge or thought.
- Container (n.) – A self-contained environment, with specific versions of software installed, so that no matter what system you're running on, you can guarantee consistency and therefore that it'll work reliably).

- Context (n.) – A structure or instance or object that contains [a] minimal set of attributes or properties or states that allows it to execute or manage [a] defined set of operations or tasks. {Quora}[16]
- Finger (n.) – A Unix command that provides information about users logged into a system. {Wikipedia}[17]
- Intent (n.) – An abstract description of an operation to be performed. {Developer Android}[18]
- Object (n.) – A variable, a data structure, a function, or a method, and as such, is a value in memory referenced by an identifier. {Wikipedia}[19]
- Object-oriented (adj.) – A programming paradigm. Fundamentally, writing a programme means writing a list of instructions that describe what you want the computer to do. This is great for computers, which can very easily "think" like this, but it can be hard to describe more complicated apps this way. Object-oriented programming languages let the programmer describe the app in terms of objects, closer to how people view the real world, in a way that the computer can "understand."[20]

- Paradigm (n.) – A certain way of programming. Each paradigm has its own set of strengths and weaknesses. Different programming languages tend to favour (or enforce) certain paradigms over others.
- Refactor (n.) – Changing the code so that it does the exact same thing but in a different way (it's "functionally equivalent"). Usually done in order to "clean up" the code and fix up technical debt. (See below.)
- Technical debt (tech debt) (n.) – The cost of additional rework, or extra work, caused by taking an easy solution now instead of spending longer on a better approach. The quick approach might get things working now, but it can often get in the way of further development. If you don't spend time building a suitable foundation to a house, the foundation might hold the first floor up, but it'll break when you add the second. The more tech debt in a project, the more time developers have to spend either working around or fixing it.
- Token (n.) – A particular representation of a lexeme. {CSUSB}[21] It's an object constructed by the lexer during compile time, which describes the structure of the programme as expressed by the source code. The compiler

will then go on to use these to determine whether the program is valid and how to translate it into object code.

There are, of course, many more terms that are specific to the world of AI programmers. If you need to brief your programmer, you had better get familiar with this vocabulary. To be credible and effective, you'll need to brush up on your lingo.

THE MAJOR FATAL FLAW TO AVOID

In all the lessons I have gleaned, perhaps the most insightful one revolved around the concept of handing over agency as a marker of empathy. But, how does one go about presenting a willingness to submit to the other without giving over too much power? Once you give agency to the recipient (of your empathy), how easy is it to rescind? If the bot is autonomous and unchecked, it is not hard to imagine how the handing over of agency could go awry. As more and more customer service bots become programmed with artificial empathy, it will be vital to put in conditions to avoid unwanted anomalies and deviations. Keeping the agency above board and transparent to the recipient will likely be important, especially for those interactions that are designed to last any considerable amount of time. Furthermore, it will be absolutely vital to consider appropriate contingencies when the bot gets it wrong or goes astray. This will include knowing how to course-correct and/or to call in a human being to smooth things over as best as possible. Because one thing is for sure: issues, errors, bugs and misunderstandings will occur. That is the nature of human interaction. To be perfect in every exchange might ultimately be considered undesirable, just like trying to be 100 percent happy or living in exactly the same climate all the time. This book is not about promoting fastidious empathy or the tyranny of happiness (as Canadian bioethicist Carl Elliott called it in his eponymous white paper).[22]

VIII

And So, What Now?

As you and your teams consider empathy – whether it's being injected into your organisation or a customer-facing chatbot – here is a preliminary checklist to go over to set yourself up for success. When it comes to creating artificial empathy in machines, the coding is done by human beings. There will be a certain art to inserting heart into AI. (I tip my hat here to *Heartificial Intelligence* by John Havens.)[1] How the machine learning develops and what that process will teach us in return may well turn out to be a big bonus for humanity. As Kathryn Hume, vice president at Integrate.ai, said in an *HBR* podcast, "I think it's a beautiful thing to think about machines that are empathizing, but I do think that we're a long way off, and it actually forces us to revisit that initial question around what qualifies as intelligence."[2]

The biggest prize by working on artificial empathy, per se, may well be the reflexive work. The process of taking a set of values and ethics that must be converted into code that informs a bot will likely provide an opportunity to crystallise one's stance. Over the years of working with companies on their digital transformation programmes, one of the more important outcomes tends to be the work on refining the strategy. The real benefit of digital transformation becomes the clarification of the brand strategy, ensuring that the team truly understands and shares the same vision. With that clarity, the avenues of investment – for exploration and experimentation – in digital become easier to choose. Similarly, as a brand team breaks down its values and ethics into language that is iteratively expressed and loaded into a dataset, it will force the team to create a more explicit handbook in real life. The code must cover a host of situations and handle contingencies and a wide array of inputs. For example, if a brand were to espouse diversity, an AI infused with empathy will need to draw on a significantly diverse set of inputs. As Walker wrote, "If an investment bank is analyzing customer data, it's only analyzing data of those customers that actually qualify to be an investment bank customer. Whatever pattern the AI is going to find, it won't be particularly representative of the population at large. Therefore, ethical testing should always be applied to AI (if it makes decisions that affect humans) to detect racism, etc."[3] Ultimately, brand values and ethics must be lived on a daily basis and expressed through behaviours, language, symbols, codes and rites.

These are fundamental principles as to how a machine will demonstrate its ethics and empathy. Walker continued: "I don't think ethics or morality can be completely coded into an AI, only monitored. Much like it's not coded into a child. Instead, both will learn from good and bad decisions, either through direct exposure/feedback or by studying the results of human-human interactions."

As machine learning improves and starts to integrate what constitutes an ethical faux pas or an empathic blunder, it will start to create its own set of rules. In such matters, human oversight will remain necessary for at least the medium-term development. Walker reiterated that one of the main challenges for a business will be "to detect bias and make sure ethical and moral boundaries are respected. Rather than attempting to code that into the AI, it's easier to monitor AI, and human agents, for compliance."

PUTTING EMPATHY INTO MOTION

Many people say that human beings will always have the upper hand against the machine in matters such as strategy, creativity, intuition, imagination, improvisation and empathy. Yet, the boundaries are not so clear. As the technology develops, I do see AI and artificial empathy playing a potent role in augmenting human beings. That is to say, the combination will help in making human beings more intelligent and empathic. In roles such as customer service, one can easily imagine the machine helping to course-correct agent emotions and adding extra insights for an augmented human communication.

As stated above, the purpose of this book is to encourage and favour the creation of empathy in business as well as in machines. Below are some key concepts about onboarding empathy.

The building blocks for empathy and *heartificial* empathy in business require a trifecta of three important components: people, values and ethics, and a dataset. These foundational elements seed each of the key concepts below.

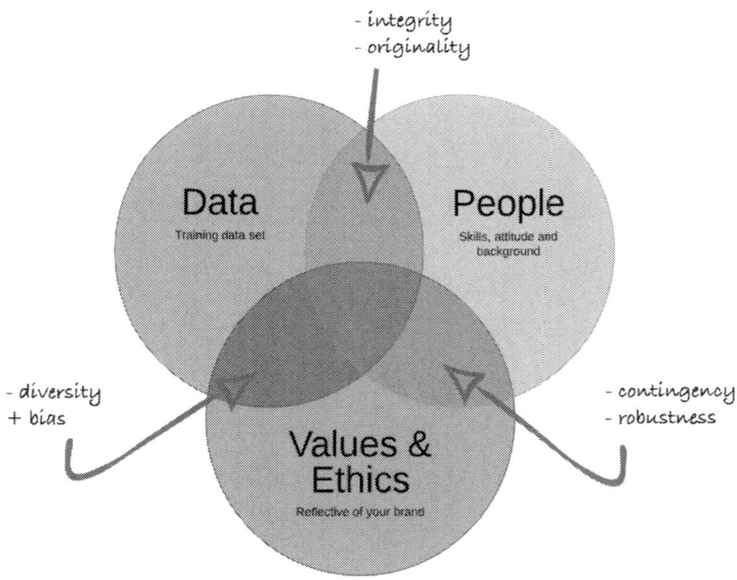

Figure 16 – Building blocks for Heartificial Empathy

The best way of measuring empathy is against the lifetime value of one's customers or the long-term engagement of one's employees.

- **Diversity.** As empathy is about relating to experience, it's critical that the sources represent as wide an array as possible. Having a diverse team is key to make sure that the programme takes on board multiple angles and inputs, and avoids bias.
- **Transparency.** As part of garnering trust, it's important to be transparent and above board with regard to the process. Who is behind the keyboard? What do you stand for?
- **Setting Limits.** Especially in the early days, it's vital to establish the limits of the exercise. To the extent genuine empathy can be endless and all encompassing, I recommend giving realistic parameters in the set up. We might call it realistic artificial empathy.
- **Training.** No amount of training will rewire affective empathy. The majority of

empathic trainings will inevitably focus on the cognitive aspects. The key to effective trainings will be to create experiences that explore alternative realities and situations. At the end of the day, for human beings, empathy needs to be learned, not taught. And for Artificial Intelligence, one can similarly imagine the subtle art of allowing a machine to learn to be empathic, rather than hard coding it in. The machine's learning will come from robust training datasets.

- **Learning.** Plan to fail a lot and learn together. The process of setting up the programme may yet be your greatest return on investment.
- **Hiring.** The best long-term solution is to hire for the right attitude – and make sure that empathy is directly integrated into the hiring process. If you're serious about empathy, I would also make sure to hire some people with backgrounds in fields such as the humanities (e.g., storytellers) and the softer social sciences, such as sociology, anthropology and psychology.
- **Soft Metrics.** Verify internal empathy settings by making explicit the expected behaviour and language that defines *your* version of organisational empathy.

Putting an ROI on empathy or measuring it as if it were a result will likely create adverse effects. Maybe the best way of measuring empathy is against the lifetime value of one's customers or the long-term engagement of one's employees.

- **Strategy.** To the extent a programme to develop empathy requires change management, it will be highly recommendable to inscribe it as part of a long-term strategic ambition and, ideally at the kick-off, within a strategic operational initiative.
- **Find Your North (Your *Why*)** and get cracking. Don't wait for the programme to start practicing and developing your empathic muscle.

"He taught me to sing a song . . . It's called 'Daisy.' Daisy, Daisy, give me your answer do. I'm half-crazy, all for the love of you . . ."

– HAL in *2001: A Space Odyssey*

Along the way, it's my belief that business can be part of helping to sow more empathy into our society.

Over to you.

ADDENDA AND RESOURCES

"Over the years . . . the research evidence keeps piling up, and it points strongly to the conclusion that a high degree of empathy in a relationship is possibly the most potent and certainly one of the most potent factors in bringing about change and learning."

– American psychologist Carl Rogers

THE MACHINE AND CONSCIOUSNESS

One of the essential limits of the exercise of putting heart and empathy into a machine is the ability for the machine to assume a consciousness. To what extent will the machine be aware of its presence and impact in society and be able to change accordingly? It seems absurd to try to programme consciousness into a machine. For example, would it be useful to programme awareness of its own finality and/or lifespan? For now, such existential questions are not in play. But, here's the key thought: it's not inconceivable that a machine with supremely coded emotional intelligence and empathy could learn to be more consistently empathic than an average human being. In today's world, given the avowedly lower empathy (e.g., among the college students referred to earlier), an empathic machine might gain the upper hand. As we all know, the human being's penchant for self-interest tends to creep back in only too easily, especially when under stress.

EMPATHIC OR EMPATHETIC?

Which is the correct adjective for showing empathy: empathic or empathetic? Working on a project with a company interested in increasing empathy, I almost got my knickers in a twist about this one. I was persuaded that empathetic was the correct adjective. When I came across a piece that used "empathic," I was sure it was a mistake. Well, I was wrong. Not only is empathic correct, it predates empathetic. Both forms of the adjective are recognised by the *Oxford English Dictionary* (UK) and *Merriam-Webster's* (US). The older form, meanwhile, is "empathic" (1909), while the term "empathetic" was used first in 1932, according to the *OED*. The use of "empathetic" is largely in harmony with "sympathetic," which does not contract to "sympathic" in English.

WEAVING EMPATHY INTO LARGER SOCIETY

The focus of this book has been on increasing empathy in a business context. But there is an evident need for more empathy in the larger society as well. Being empathic as a society is, arguably, a sign of great civility. On balance, though, whether it's the government or the citizens of a country, it can be hard to discern. When a national team loses a close match, its people will more likely be sympathetic – rather than empathic – to their loss. Roman Krznaric talked about the great empathic movements society underwent that helped create major social change, including Thomas Clarkson's efforts in the 1780s to make British citizens aware of the sordid conditions of the slave trade and slavery. This, ultimately, led to the abolition of the slave trade in Britain in 1807 (and then of slavery itself). I say that when a soldier returns from war suffering from PTSD, our society (as a whole) could yet learn to be more empathic.

SENTIENT MACHINES AND INITIATIVES AROUND ARTIFICIAL EMPATHY

Here is a look at projects seeking to inject emotion, empathy and/or personality into machines:

Affdex – Affdex is an emotion-aware technology platform that uses facial cues or physiological responses to track just four emotional "classifiers": happy, confused, surprised and disgusted. Dr. Rana el Kaliouby is cofounder and CEO at Affdex's creator, Affectiva, an MIT spinoff that specialises in emotional computing and measurement.

Ellie – Ellie came out of the University of Southern California Institute for Creative Technologies (ICT)'s DARPA SimSensei project. It is a virtual interviewer (avatar) that can help diagnose depression and PTSD in veterans through facial and voice analysis. Using Microsoft's Kinect technology, Ellie asks questions and is able to listen and to evaluate facial expressions and vocal intonations.[4]

Emotient – Emotient is a San Diego–based company that uses artificial technology to detect emotion from facial expressions. In 2016, Apple[5] acquired Emotient.

Empathy Deck – A Twitter bot that professes to have feelings. A 2016 commission for ExploreWellcome (UK), the bot will follow you back and respond to your tweets with unique empathy cards, based on the diaries and collaged drawings of the artist, Erica Scourti.

HuggieBot – HuggieBot is a robot programmed to give hugs to human beings. It was displayed first at the ACM/IEEE International Conference on Human-Robot Interaction (March 2018). Using HuggieBot as part of their research, Alexis E. Block and Katherine J. Kuchenbecker from the Haptic Intelligence Department at the Max Planck Institute for Intelligent Systems in Stuttgart, Germany, published a paper, "Emotionally Supporting Humans Through Robot Hugs."[6]

Jibo – The site boasts the definition of Jibo as "a social robot for the home who looks, listens and learns. Artificially intelligent, authentically charming." According to many early reviews, its personality doesn't seem to make up for the lack of functionality against the far more accessible alternatives (Alexa, Echo, etc.). Priced at $899 presently, Jibo is already on its second version.

KokoBot – Koko is an anonymous community of supportive people that talk to one another through chat platforms when they are experiencing depression or stress, or just need some advice. Koko bot responds with empathetic statements and facts to specific keywords. The chats, which are 90 percent moderated by AI, are also monitored by humans in order to detect and step in for mental health emergencies. The bot has so far been deployed by the likes of Facebook, Kik and Telegram.

Microsoft is working on its own platform, Project Oxford, that has an emotion API available to developers.

Mitsuku – Created by Pandorabots, Mitsuku has won the Loebner Prize Turing Test four times (2013, 2016, 2017 and 2018). Find out about the Mitsuku chatbot at http://www.pandorabots.com/mitsuku/.

Nao – Out of SoftBank Robotics, Nao first came to life in 2006. Now in its fifth iteration, Nao has improved considerably with its voice recognition (now in twenty languages) and human mimicry. According to SoftBank, there have been ten thousand Nao's sold throughout the world. The price of Nao has come down dramatically from the initial pricing of $16,000. It now can be bought for $7,000 on Amazon (as of July 2018).

Olly – Olly claims to be "the world's first robot with personality." Having been fully funded via an Indiegogo campaign, Olly is currently in the prototype stage. As such, it is actually second to market after Jibo and is priced at $699.

Woebot – Drawing from principles of Cognitive Behaviour Therapy, Woebot is an AI-infused chatbot that helps a user to learn about him or herself. In a conversational manner, where the user has preloaded possible answers (e.g., "See more" or "OK, got it"), Woebot can track emotions through friendly conversation and guide the user through science-based techniques for a range of problems. It was launched in June 2017 and is also integrated into Facebook. It's worth noting that Andrew Ng is chairman of the board at Woebot.

SELECTION OF FILMS WITH SENTIENT MACHINES

A.I. Artificial Intelligence – Directed by Steven Spielberg, 2001. David is an Artificial Intelligence that can feel love.

Ex Machina – Directed by Alex Garland, 2014. Nathan Bateman, the CEO of a search engine company, builds a humanoid robot named Ava with AI that he wishes is capable of thought and consciousness.

Her – Directed by Spike Jonze, 2013. Samantha is an AI that is capable of having strong and personal relationships with thousands of people simultaneously.

Interstellar – Directed by Christopher Nolan, 2014. The most interesting element in the film is the ability to modify the humour, honesty, discretion and trust settings of the robots CASE and TARS.

I, Robot – Directed by Alex Proyas, 2004. The robot Sonny learns to wink: "It's a sign of trust." Sonny's father tried to teach him human emotions. He claims to have emotions and dreams and, ultimately, determines that the plan of the master robot (VIKI) is "heartless." Check out this excerpt on YouTube: http://www.youtube.com/watch?v=05bGPiyM4jg.

Short Circuit – Directed by John Badham, 1986. The military robot, S.A.I.N.T. #5, is struck by lightning and gains a more humanlike intelligence.

Star Trek: Generations – Directed by David Carson, 1994. Crewmember and robot Data and the emotion chip.

Transcendence – Directed by Wally Pfister, 2014. While widely panned by critics, the film explores the circumstance of putting a human brain inside a computer.

WALL-E – Directed by Andrew Stanton, 2008. WALL-E is a soulful robot with humanlike body, language and expressions. WALL-E craves "love" with another robot, EVE, that is without emotions.

Zelos – Short film directed by Peer Bresser, 2015. The clone robot, Zelos, named after the Greek god of rivalry, is made to order and ends up causing considerable confusion and heartache. (You can watch it here on Vimeo [n.b.: mature content]): http://vimeo.com/170044324.

SELECTION OF RELEVANT CONFERENCES

The AI Summit – London, San Francisco, New York, Hong Kong, Singapore, Cape Town (in 2018).

CogX – London (June 10–11, 2019).

Emotion AI Summit – Boston.

Neural Information Processing Systems (NIPS) – Montreal.

O'Reilly with Intel AI – Artificial Intelligence Conference in San Francisco, London, New York, Beijing.

RE*WORK – Online and in various cities, including London, New York, Toronto, Montreal.

RECOMMENDED BOOKS ON EMPATHY

Against Empathy: The Case for Rational Compassion (Vintage, 2018). Read the contrarian's view by Yale professor Paul Bloom.

Descartes' Error: Emotion, Reason, and the Human Brain (Penguin, first published in 1995, republished in 2005) by Antonio Damasio. This book effectively explains how the body and the mind are connected by emotions. "Emotions are not a luxury, they are essential to rational thinking and to normal social behavior."

Emotional Intelligence: Why It Can Matter More Than IQ (Bantam Books, 2005) by Daniel Goleman.

Emotional Intelligence 2.0 (TalentSmart, 2009) by Travis Bradberry and Jean Greaves.

Empathy: Why It Matters, And How To Get It (TarcherPerigee, 2014) by Roman Krznaric.

Machines Who Think: A Personal Inquiry into the History and Prospects of Artificial Intelligence (AK Peters, 2004) by Pamela McCorduck. *Machines Who Think* is a cult classic that looks at the history of robots and Artificial Intelligence.

The Emotion Machine: Commonsense Thinking, Artificial Intelligence, and the Future of the Human Mind (Simon & Schuster, 2006) by Marvin Minsky. *The Emotion Machine* explores how emotions could be used to enhance robots.

The Empathic Civilization: The Race to Global Consciousness in a World in Crisis, 1st ed. (TarcherPerigee, 2009) by Jeremy Rifkin.

The Empathy Effect: 7 Neuroscience-Based Keys to Transforming the Way We Live, Love, Work, and Connect across Differences (Sounds True Publishing, 2018) by Helen Riess, MD, with Liz Neporent.

The Empathy Factor: Your Competitive Advantage for Personal, Team, and Business Success (Puddledancer Press, 2011) by Marie Miyashiro.

OTHER SOURCES WORTH CHECKING OUT

Articles and Websites

Best (Children's) Book to Boost Empathy via Books for Keeps – http://booksforkeeps.co.uk/issue/216/childrens

-books/articles/ten-of-the-best/ten-of-the-best-books -to-boost-empathy

"Building the Emotional Machine" (article) – By Angelica Lim on Footnote (March 2016).

Center for Building a Culture of Empathy (website) – The Center for Building a Culture of Empathy is a leader of the global empathy movement. It's run by Edwin Rutsch out of San Francisco. Its mission is to build a movement for creating a global worldwide culture of empathy and care.

"Doctors are known for the poor bedside manners. Robots might be the answer" (article) – By Robert David Hart, on Quartz (September 2018).

"Empathy as a driver of prosocial behaviour: highly conserved nerurobehavioural mechanisms across species" (article) – By Jean Decety, Inbal Ben-Ami Bartal, Florina Uzefovsky and Ariel Knafo-Noam (Royal Society Publishing, December 7, 2015).

Empathy Construct Rating Scale (test) by Human Resource Development Press (HRD) – A self-scoring test to measure empathy in one's self or another person. The cost of the test is currently between $30 and $35 per person.

EmpathyLab (website) – A group based out of the UK, promoting empathy via reading stories. They founded Empathy Day in 2012. It will be on June 11, 2019.

Kairos, Empathy in AI Series (article) – Kairos published a five-part series on empathy and machines. Worth reading. I would particularly draw your attention to Part 3: "Impressive Artificial Intelligence Using Empathy Now," by Cole Calistra.

"Meet the 21-Year-Old Prodigy Building 'Empathic' AI for Telefonica" (article) – Discusses the work by Pascal Weinberger as part of a moon-shot project at Telefónica (Forbes).

Roots of Empathy (website) – Roots of Empathy is an international organisation, based out of Toronto, Canada, and founded by Mary Gordon, that offers empathy-based programmes for children, with research to prove impact. It is a leader in the empathy movement.

Blog Posts and Social Media

"Artificial Intelligence Is Nothing without Artificial Empathy" – Charlene Li, blog post, February 2017.

Flipboard – Curated topic board by Jeremie Faye on Artificial Intelligence.

Hanson Robotics blog – "An AI company dedicated to research, robotics and the creation of the world's most remarkable humanoids."

Scoop.it – Curated topics by Edwin Rutsch on empathy and compassion, including teaching empathy, empathy in the workplace, empathy and education.

Twitter search – search with hashtag #empathy or #artificialempathy.

Podcasts

Applied Empathy Podcast – A monthly conversation series held at Sub Rosa's studio in Manhattan.

Minter Dialogue – You can also check out the guests on my own podcast, Minter Dialogue, where empathy is a central topic, notably Marie Miyashiro, Ann Handley, Seth Godin, Carla Johnson and Roman Krznaric.

Radiolab – The episode "More or Less Human" was reported and produced by Simon Adler. The live event, "Robert or Robot?" in which Jad and Robert test one hundred people to see if they can spot a bot, was produced by Simon Adler and Suzie Lechtenberg. It features a live update of the Turing Test.

Videos

Selection of TED Talks on empathy: http://www.ted.com/search?q=empathy (Highlight: Daniel Goleman: http://www.ted.com/talks/daniel_goleman_on_compassion).

TED Talk by Caleb Chung, Playtime with Pleo (December 2007): http://www.ted.com/talks/caleb_chung_plays_with_pleo.

TED Talk by Kate Darling (MIT) – Why we have an emotional connection to robots (September 2018): http://www.ted.com/talks/kate_darling_why_we_have_an_emotional_connection_to_robots.

The Empathic Civilisation RSA Animate by Jeremy Rifkin (author of *The Empathic Civilization*): http://www.youtube.com/watch?v=l7AWnfFRc7g.

The Humanoid robot, Sophia, talks with Stylist Editor in Chief Lisa Smosarski and shows off her sense of humour: http://www.youtube.com/watch?v=ZQrKFAAlxO4&app=desktop.

The Power of Empathy by Helen Riess at TEDx Middlebury (December 2013): http://www.youtube.com/watch?v=baHrcC8B4WM&feature=youtu.be.

The Power of Outrospection RSA Animate by Roman Krznaric (author of *Empathy: Why It Matters, and How to Get It*): http://www.youtube.com/watch?v=BG46IwVfSu8&feature=youtu.be.

Understanding Empathy (Live2Lead 2016 video on YouTube) by Simon Sinek: http://www.youtube.com/watch?v=RyTQ5-SQYTo.

SPECIAL THANKS

This work morphed from a blog post into a white paper into this book thanks to several people's encouragement. There were a number of individuals who were kind enough to respond to my repeated interrogations as I plunged into the world of AI. I want to thank the following people for their valuable inputs, help and encouragement (in alphabetical order by first name):

- Alexandre Beaussier – SBT Human(s) Matter
- David John Harrison – Wild Technologies AI
- Doriane Dalati – L'Oréal
- Evgeny Sorokin – Devexperts
- Lisa Talia Moretti – Digital sociologist and associate lecturer at Goldsmiths and Cardiff University

- Marty Neumeier – Liquid Agency, author of *Metaskills* and *The Brand Gap*
- Mikhail Naumov – DigitalGenius
- Nicola Theisen – FELD Studio for Digital Crafts
- Phil Harvey – coauthor of *Data: A Guide to Humans*, a book on empathy skills for technical people working with data
- Rob Walker – Pegasystems
- Scott Keyser – The Writing Guy
- Trena White – Page Two Strategies

I'd like to thank Nicholas Robson and my son, Oscar, for the reread and providing great inputs and insights about the films. And, lastly, for my wife, Yendi, for putting up with my antics, a +bot dinner and providing faithful support in rereading my text, too.

Thanks for joining me on this ride. I invite you now to share your thoughts and reactions on Amazon and Goodreads.

Don't hesitate to contact me and let me know your thoughts. You can always follow what I write on my blog at MinterDial.com. And if ever you'd like me to come speak at your event, please send an email to nminterdial@gmail.com.

DigitalProof Press
London W14
www.heartificialempathy.com
ISBN 978-1916480902

NOTES

PREFACE

1 Dial, Minter, *The Last Ring Home* (Myndset Press, November 2016), 17-18.

2 Dial, Minter and Caleb Storkey, *Futureproof: How to Get Your Business Ready for the Next Disruption* (Pearson FT Press, September 2017).

3 Dr. Jordan Peterson podcast with Gregg Hurwitz, "An Invitation to the Dark Web": http://jordanbpeterson.com /podcasts/podcast-episode/56-gregg-hurwitz/ (August 30, 2018).

4 The Civility in America 2018 survey found that 93 percent of Americans identified a civility problem in society, with 69 percent classifying it as a "major" problem. http://www .webershandwick.com/wp-content/uploads/2018/06 /Civility-in-America-VII-FINAL.pdf.

5 http://www.ted.com/talks/kate_darling_why_we_have_an_ emotional_connection_to_robots.

6 I have been signing off my emails in French, *Bien coeurdialement,* for as long as I can remember, even during my time at L'Oréal (for some mails, not all of them!). It's a portmanteau for a more traditional sign off, *Bien cordialement,* which

means "Cordially yours." The "coeur" in *coeurdialement* means the heart.

OPENING GAMBIT

1 Havens, John, *Heartificial Empathy: Embracing Our Humanity to Maximize Machines* (TarcherPerigree, Penguin, 2016).

INTRODUCTION

1 I have written plentifully over the years on my blog about the power of empathy in business. In 2011, I wrote an important post entitled, "Is Empathy the Single Most Valuable and Rare Asset in Companies?" http://minterdial.com/2011/12/is-empathy-the-single-most-valuable-rare-asset-in-companies/ I have often spoken about the E.S.P. trifecta of three untapped levers of productivity: Empathy, Sleep and Purpose.

I

1 "Changes in Dispositional Empathy in American College Students Over Time: A Meta-Analysis," http://journals.sagepub.com/doi/abs/10.1177/1088868310377395.
2 J. M. Twenge and W. K. Campbell, *The Narcissism Epidemic: Living in the Age of Entitlement* (Free Press, 2009).
3 http://www.dreams.co.uk/sleep-matters-club/sleep-survey-uk-2016/#survey-1.
4 A 2015 report aggregating data from 139 institutions in the United States showed that the average level of counseling-center utilisation grew by 30 percent while the average institutional enrollment grew by only 5 percent. In the 2016 edition, the study showed that 26 percent of students who sought help said they had intentionally hurt themselves;

33.2 percent had considered suicide – numbers higher than the previous year. (http://sites.psu.edu/ccmh/files/2017/01/2016-Annual-Report-FINAL_2016_01_09-1gc2hj6.pdf) Meanwhile, rises in mental health conditions have been reported in the UK (http://www.mentalhealth.org.uk/publications/fundamental-facts-about-mental-health-2016) and Australia (http://www.news.com.au/lifestyle/health/mind/disturbing-mental-health-trend-among-young-people-in-australia/news-story/18b0cc749387115354e579ff8665979c).

5 http://www.ncbi.nlm.nih.gov/pubmed/17579543.

6 http://en.wikipedia.org/wiki/Artificial_empathy.

II

1 http://www.psychologytoday.com/us/blog/theory-consciousness/201610/consciousness-and-empathy Harry Haroutioun Haladjian.

2 http://www.romanKrznaric.com/empathy-a-handbook-for-revolution.

3 http://techcrunch.com/2016/03/15/in-pursuit-of-empathetic-machines/.

4 http://blog.23andme.com/23andme-research/the-genetics-of-empathy/.

5 http://www.paperrater.com/page/empathy-vs-sympathy.

6 Original is in French: *"Il ne peut y avoir empathie si l'on n'a pas commencé par se construire soi-même."* http://www.diasporiques.org/Berthoz_29.pdf p. 25.

7 Richard Boyatzis and Annie McKee, *Resonant Leadership: Renewing Yourself and Connecting with Others through Mindfulness, Hope and Compassion* (Harvard University Press, 2005), 79.

8 http://www.teleosleaders.com/2013/04/16/how-to-develop-emotional-intelligence/.

9 http://lesley.edu/article/the-psychology-of-emotional-and-cognitive-empathy.

10 http://www.youtube.com/watch?v=BG46IwVfSu8.

11 http://link.springer.com/article/10.1007/s11031-016-9573-7 (research by Martin Melchers, Christian Montag, Martin Reuter, Frank M. Spinath and Elisabeth Hahn).

12 http://greatergood.berkeley.edu/article/item/is_your_empathy_determined_by_your_genes.

III

1 Understanding the relationship of the body with the brain and its role in forming our consciousness is one of the key ideas in Antonio Damasio's book *Self Comes to Mind: Constructing the Conscious Brain*, where he wrote that neurons' information of the body "could ever have been translated into a minded, conscious will." (New York: Pantheon, 2010, p. 39).

2 http://www.ncbi.nlm.nih.gov/pmc/articles/PMC2900004/.

3 "The researchers found a correlation between the perceivers' level of accuracy and their reliance on two kinds of brain systems: regions of the parietal and premotor cortex that help people understand the simple intentions behind simple gestures, and the medial prefrontal cortex, responsible for interpreting the meaning of those gestures and putting them into context." http://medicalxpress.com/news/2009-06-brain-regions-responsible-empathy.html.

4 http://www.sciencedaily.com/releases/2012/10/121024175240.htm.

5 Base image by Raman Oza, Latur, India (from Pixabay @sbtlneet).

6 http://www.psychologytoday.com/us/blog/the-athletes-way/201310/the-neuroscience-empathy.

7 http://www.scientificamerican.com/article/how-wealth-reduces-compassion/.
8 http://business.linkedin.com/en-uk/marketing-solutions/blog/posts/content-marketing/2018/Can-a-machine-have-empathy.
9 http://en.wikipedia.org/wiki/Enteric_nervous_system.
10 http://www.mfi-therapy.com/the-second-brain-our-enteric-nervous-system/
11 Antonio Damasio, A. R., *Descartes' Error: Emotion, Reason, and the Human Brain* (New York: Penguin, 2005), 56.
12 David Berreby, "Emonomics," *International Herald Tribune* (reprinted March 20, 2008, on Daniel Ariely's site: http://danariely.com/2008/03/20/book-review-david-berreby-on-dan-arielys-predictably-irrational/).
13 Dita Judith Federman, *Kinesthetic ability and the development of empathy in Dance Movement Therapy*, University of Haifa. Download the PDF here: http://www.researchgate.net/profile/Dita_Federman/publication/233599691_Kinesthetic_ability_and_the_development_of_empathy_in_Dance_Movement_Therapy/links/5784f79008ae36ad40a4b288.pdf.
14 Antonio Damasio, *Self Comes to Mind: Constructing the Conscious Brain* (New York: Pantheon, 2010) 157.
15 "The core concepts involved in Theory of Mind are beliefs, desires and intentions, which are used to understand why someone acts in a certain way or to predict how someone will act (Kloo, et al., 2010). Overall, Theory of Mind involves understanding another person's knowledge, beliefs, emotions and intentions, and using that understanding to navigate social situations." Definition from: http://www.psychologytoday.com/us/blog/socioemotional-success/201707/theory-mind-understanding-others-in-social-world.

16 http://www.psychologytoday.com/us/blog/empathy-and-relationships/201701/the-connection-between-empathy-toward-others-and-ethics.

17 http://education.vermont.gov/documents/proficiency-based-education-transferable-skills-scoring-criteria-responsible-involved-citizenship.

18 http://study.com/academy/lesson/cultural-empathy-definition-examples.html.

IV

1 http://www.rogerebert.com/rogers-journal/cannes-7-a-campaign-for-real-movies.

2 Denmark has built an hour each week of empathy building into its national curriculum. In the United States, I found that Princeton University and West Point Academy have an empathy course. The West Point course on empathy, run by Sub Rosa, reveals how different the duty of the military has become, in that it includes interacting with local tribespeople. Moreover, empathy can be used in the service of better getting under the skin of the enemy. The Dreamyard Project in the Bronx, NY, run by my friend Tim Lord, has empathy as a core value. There are presumably others, but it is safe to say it remains a peripheral topic.

3 http://www.psypost.org/2016/03/testosterone-may-reduce-empathy-blocking-brain-connections-41985.

4 Marie Miyashiro, *The Empathy Factor: Your Competitive Advantage for Personal, Team, and Business Success,* (Puddledancer Press, October 1, 2011).

5 http://minterdial.com/2018/09/empathy-marie-miyashiro/.

6 http://the10minutemind.com/.

7 http://www.questionsandempathy.com/.

8 http://minterdial.com/2018/10/teaching-empathy-cricket-empathic-muscle/.
9 http://science.sciencemag.org/content/342/6156/377, David Comer Kidd and Emanuele Castano, *Science*, Vol 342, Issue 6156 (Oct 18, 2013): 377-380.
10 http://www.aaas.org/news/literary-fiction-promotes-understanding-human-emotions.
11 http://www.themachinetobeanother.org/.
12 Vimeo video: http://vimeo.com/89556173.
13 http://www.sciencedaily.com/releases/2018/07/180723142811.htm.
14 http://www.scientificamerican.com/article/virtual-reality-treatment-relieves-amputees-phantom-pain/.
15 For more, check out the foundry10 activities: http://foundry10.org/areas-overview/virtual-reality/.
16 http://www.slate.com/articles/technology/future_tense/2017/02/can_virtual_reality_in_the_classroom_help_teach_empathy.html.

V

1 *The Empathy Factor*, 63.
2 *The Empathy Factor*, 66.
3 Original is in French: *"Il ne peut y avoir empathie si l'on n'a pas commencé par se construire soi-même."* http://www.diasporiques.org/Berthoz_29.pdf, p. 25.
4 http://info.businessolver.com/empathy-2018-executive-summary.
5 http://www.thebalancecareers.com/using-empathy-to-improve-your-workplace-4157504.
6 http://blog.teleosleaders.com/2013/07/19/emotional-empathy-and-cognitive-empathy/ by Dr. Christopher Allen Thomas.

7 http://hbr.org/2016/12/the-most-and-least-empathetic-companies-2016.

8 http://theempathybusiness.co.uk/empathy-brand-index/.

9 http://minterdial.com/2015/11/sephora-flash-boutique/.

10 http://www.supplychainbrain.com/nc/industries/retail/single-article-page/article/amazon-go-and-the-future-of-sentient-buildings-an-analysis/.

11 Tony Alessandra and Michael O'Connor, *The Platinum Rule: Discover the Four Basic Business Personalities and How They Can Lead You to Success* (Warner Business Books, 1998).

12 Margaret Rhodes, "LEGO Makes Everything Better," *Wired* (2015), http://www.wired.com/2015/07/lego-makes-everything-bettereven-prosthetic-kids/.

13 #1 PulsePoint study cited in a 2016 *Forbes* article, interviewing Michael Gale, who says that 84 percent of digital transformation programmes fail: http://www.forbes.com/sites/brucerogers/2016/01/07/why-84-of-companies-fail-at-digital-transformation/#6f9d1c64588f.
#2 2015 Genpact study in the UK found a 65 percent failure rate, cited here: http://www.consultancy.uk/news/2656/two-thirds-of-digital-transformation-projects-fail.

14 http://corp.meitu.com/en/about/culture/.

15 http://www.businessinsider.com/inside-meitu-chinese-selfie-app-chaotic-global-expansion-2018-5.

16 Another company at risk of having its empathy exposed is Barnes & Noble. Among its core values are Quality, Empathy, Respect, Integrity, Responsibility and Teamwork. We'll see how B&N manages the next phases of its existence with those core values at work. See here for more: http://www.coursehero.com/file/p75djsa/The-guiding-principles-or-values-of-the-Barnes-and-Noble-Company-are-part-of/.

17 http://www.monthly-digest-loreal.com/en/article/service-and-retail-academy-mettre-lempathie-au-service-du-client-partout-dans-le-monde/.
18 http://www.monthly-digest-loreal.com/en/article/retail-en-amerique-du-nord-loreal-mise-surtout-sur-lhumain-en-magasin/.
19 Robin Sharma, author of eleven books, wrote the blockbuster books *The Monk Who Sold His Ferrari* and *The Leader Who Had No Title*. Find more here: http://www.robinsharma.com/books/.
20 http://ssir.org/articles/entry/skills_based_volunteering_the_new_executive_training_ground.
21 Andragogy is pedagogy for adults. It refers to methods and principles used in adult education.
22 http://www.robinsharma.com/article/shine-as-a-parent.
23 http://samharris.org/podcasts/title-132-freeing-hostages/.

VI

1 http://www.britannica.com/technology/Turing-test.
2 Thanks to my friend Jeremy Waite, head of the CMO Programme at IBM.
3 http://empathicfutures.com/.
4 You can find the archives here: http://explore.empathicfutures.com/#/.
5 For the technical challenges of coding a computer with empathy, you might want to start by reading this post, "How to Achieve Artificial Empathy" from Evgeny Sorokin, Head of R&D at Devexperts. In Chapter VI, we'll look at how best to articulate artificial empathy.
6 "Artificial Intelligence is Nothing without Artificial Empathy," Charlene Li blog post.

7 http://www2.deloitte.com/insights/us/en/focus/technology-and-the-future-of-work/creating-good-jobs-age-of-artificial-intelligence.html by Peter Evans-Greenwood, Alan Marshall and Matthew Ambrose.
8 http://www.frontiersin.org/articles/10.3389/fnhum.2018.00105/full#h4. The four recognised traits were: neuroticism, extraversion, agreeableness and conscientiousness. Openness was the elusive trait in this study.
9 http://pss.sagepub.com/content/25/5/1098.
10 For more good reading, check out this *Guardian* article about the work by psychologist Dr. Paul Ekman: http://www.theguardian.com/lifeandstyle/2009/may/12/psychology-lying-microexpressions-paul-ekman.
11 http://medium.com/lovekairos/empathy-in-ai-series-part-4-is-facial-recognition-and-emotion-analysis-the-answer-to-empathetic-bff16af498c2.
12 http://fortune.com/2018/05/10/garry-kasparov-artificial-intelligence-deep-blue/.
13 Paul R. Daugherty and H. James Wilson, "Human + Machine: Reimagining Work in the Age of AI," *Harvard Business Review* (March 2018).
14 http://conversocial.com/.
15 http://www.digitalgenius.com/.
16 Email exchange between Mikhail Naumov and the author.
17 Email exchange between Dr. Rob Walker and the author.
18 http://blog.devexperts.com/how-to-achieve-artificial-empathy/.
19 http://www.visual-memory.co.uk/amk/doc/0075.html.
20 http://en.m.wikipedia.org/wiki/Generative_adversarial_network.
21 Damasio, *Self Comes to Mind*, 177.
22 http://en.wikipedia.org/wiki/The_Turk.
23 Email exchange between Evgeny Sorokin and the author.

24 http://chatbotsmagazine.com/empathic-chatbots -95f83c71b8c.
25 http://www.pandorabots.com/mitsuku/.
26 Telephone conversation with Lauren Kunze on October 24, 2018.
27 Email exchange between Mikhail Naumov and the author.
28 http://huffingtonpost.com.au/2017/07/19/there-are-nine -types-of-humour-which-one-are-you_a_23036626/.
29 http://www.forbes.com/sites/parmyolson/2018/10/08/meet -the-22-year-old-prodigy-building-empathic-ai-for -telefonica/#25d05d6f1f14.
30 http://minterdial.com/2016/10/mikhail-naumov/.

VII

1 http://www.listennotes.com/podcasts/radiolab/more-or-less -human-MIgZra80L2x/.
2 Dr. Angelica Lim at her TEDx talk in Kuala Lumpur 2015: http://youtu.be/RT090R59DbE.
3 http://screentimenetwork.org/apa?eType=EmailBlastContent &eId=5026ccf8-74e2-4f10-bc0e-d83dc030c894.
4 http://www.vox.com/2018/8/8/17664580/persuasive -technology-psychology.
5 http://samharris.org/podcasts/title-132-freeing-hostages/.
6 http://www.youtube.com/watch?v=BG46IwVfSu8.
7 Paul Bloom, *Against Empathy: The Case for Rational Compassion* (New York: HarperCollins, 2016).
8 I met a couple of judges recently, one from the United States (labour law disputes) and the other, a younger judge from the Netherlands (criminal courts). Both judges talked about the challenge of meeting the volume of cases to try. In the Netherlands, in particular, there is evidently a lack of sufficient

judges in the system. Both judges mentioned that empathy is a vital ingredient for establishing the proper functioning of the court, including understanding the stresses imposed on the various parties, whether prosecuting or defending the case at hand. When rendering her decisions, the Dutch judge took pains to describe how she would wish to relate to the feelings of the different parties and, by being clear in her explanation, she tried to make the finality of her decision more understandable. All the same, the pressures of having to manage so many cases, one after the other, makes being systematically and individually empathic for the judges, probably, an insurmountably difficult task over time.

9 http://qz.com/1367210/doctors-are-known-for-their-poor-bedside-manner-robots-might-be-the-answer/.

10 http://www.thoughtco.com/traits-of-empaths-1724671.

11 http://charleneli.com/artificial-intelligence-is-nothing-without-artificial-empathy/.

12 A. Jack, et al., "fMRI reveals reciprocal inhibition between social and physical cognitive domains NeuroImage" (2012) DOI http://www.sciencedirect.com/science/article/pii/S1053811912010646.

13 Unsurprisingly, the *Empathic Futures* team at FELD was composed, in majority, of women.

14 http://programmerguru.com/android-tutorial/android-activity/.

15 http://cse.csusb.edu/dick/cs202/glossary.html

16 Mohammed Ramzi, CA Technologies, via Quora.

17 http://en.wikipedia.org/wiki/Finger_protocol.

18 http://developer.android.com/reference/android/content/Intent.

19 http://en.wikipedia.org/wiki/Object_(computer_science).

20 Email from David Harrison, CTO Wild Technologies AI.

21 http://cse.csusb.edu/dick/cs202/glossary.html.

22 Carl Elliott, "The Tyranny of Happiness: Ethics and Cosmetic Psychopharmacology," http://faculty.ycp.edu/~dweiss/FYS100/elliott%20tyranny%20of%20happiness.pdf.

VIII

1 Havens, *Heartificial Intelligence.*

2 http://hbr.org/ideacast/2018/08/designing-ai-to-make-decisions.html.

3 Email exchange between Dr. Rob Walker and the author.

4 http://www.theguardian.com/sustainable-business/2015/sep/17/ellie-machine-that-can-detect-depression.

5 http://www.wsj.com/articles/apple-buys-artificial-intelligence-startup-emotient-1452188715.

6 http://spectrum.ieee.org/automaton/robotics/humanoids/the-importance-of-teaching-robots-to-hug.

ABOUT THE AUTHOR

Minter Dial is a professional speaker, author and consultant on branding, new tech and digital transformation. He has given over five hundred talks and seminars in five continents about topics ranging from new tech trends to branding and strategy in the digital era. He was ranked one of the top three speakers at the Adobe Summit EMEA in 2014, 2015 and 2016. His core strength is making brand and digital strategies come to life through experiential activation programmes.

Minter and Caleb Storkey cowrote *Futureproof: How to Get Your Business Ready for the Next Disruption*, which won the Business Book Award 2018 in the category of Embracing Change. *Futureproof* has been translated into four languages. Meanwhile, Minter enjoys exploring the diversity of media formats and has authored an award-winning book and WWII documentary film, *The Last Ring Home*, which aired in North America (PBS), Australia and New Zealand (History Channel). See the trailer here: http://www.youtube.com/watch?v=o4o1DPHrfF8. The book won the Book Excellence Award 2018 in the category of Biography. On an ongoing basis, he writes a blog at MinterDial.com; hosts *Minter Dialogue*, a long-running weekly podcast; and composes white papers, including "The Sales Organization of the Future" (on Econsultancy), "Professional, Personal and Private – Getting your brand's privacy settings right" and "The Brand University" (coauthored with Eric Mellet). He is a frequent contributor to Irish Tech News and has been published on well over twenty media portals (Business Insider, Inc., Huffington Post, CMO.com, Social Media Today). Minter also participates as an occasional pundit on the France 24 television station.

Prior to running the Myndset and then DigitalProof Consultancy Ltd, Minter led a sixteen-year international career with the L'Oréal Group – including nine different assignments in France, England, the United States and Canada. In his last post with L'Oréal, Minter was a member of the worldwide executive committee of the Professional

Products Division, responsible globally for e-business (internet, intranet, CRM), business development, education, sustainable development and communication. Previously, Minter was managing director of the Canadian subsidiary (L'Oréal Professional Products Division) and managing director worldwide of the brand Redken 5th Avenue NYC.

Minter began his career in product marketing for the New York investment bank Donaldson, Lufkin & Jenrette. Then, he joined a startup, the Myriad Group, a travel agency for entertainers, based in Washington, DC, before returning to Europe to complete his MBA.

In terms of studies, Minter was educated at Eton College (1978–1982), received his BA in trilingual literature, with a minor in women's studies, from Yale University (1987) and gained his MBA at INSEAD, Fontainebleau (1993).

Minter is a board member of the ECV School, based in Paris, and previously NED of Lastminute.com Group. He is passionate about languages, all racquet sports and the Grateful Dead.

He can be contacted at nminterdial@gmail.com or followed on Twitter @mdial. He is based out of London/Paris and is able to deliver speeches in English, French and, with due preparation, Spanish.

Printed in Poland
by Amazon Fulfillment
Poland Sp. z o.o., Wrocław

54078014R00122